Death Sucks

A Straight-Up Guide to Navigating Your Pet's Final Transition

By *Alexa Linton*

With contributions from
Celeste Morris and Bradley Morris

Front and back cover photos of Cathy Hamilton and her dog, Truffles and pictures of Alexa and Kia the dog by photographer Devon Gillott. Book and cover design by Alexa Linton.

Editor: Kari Magnuson

Linton, Alexa
  Death Sucks: A Straight-Up Guide to Navigating Your Pet's Final Transition / Alexa Linton
ISBN: 978-0-9951504-0-9

1st edition, March 2016

Ebook ISBN: 978-0-9951504-1-6

Contents

This book was created to support animal lovers and stewards in the final transition of their animal companions. My hope is that something in the coming pages will provide you comfort, insight and perhaps even an opportunity to see things differently. Yes, death and dying sucks, particularly the loss of a beloved animal companion. It can be a time marked by profound sadness and loss, and as you're about to discover, it can also be an experience filled with tremendous learning and growth. It is a multi-faceted experience, marked by layers and levels of past and present experiences and real or perceived trauma and pain, potentially amplifying the heartbreak of current events or those challenging ones that inevitably lie in our future. Healing through these layers can birth a new level of understanding and a greater clarity in our perception, as we're about to find out. This journey will be unique to each individual, affected by their past, their present, their future and, of course, the unique connection with their beloved animal.

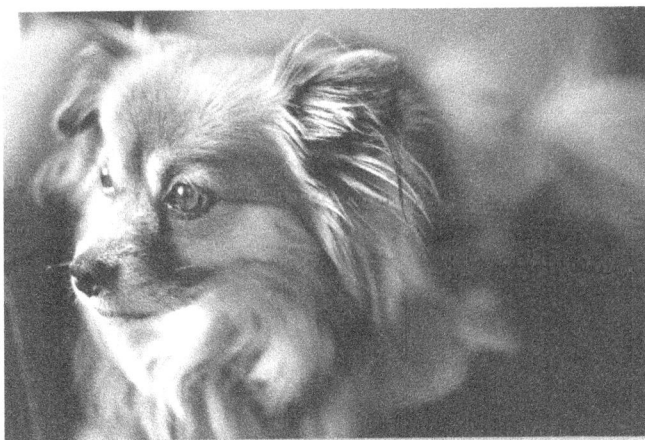

Gratitude for Animals

I would love to take a moment now, before we begin, to honour all of the animals who have graced our lives—those who are still with us, those who are to come and those who have made their transition. These incredible beings are our teachers, friends and family and bring us closer to the truth of who we are if we allow it. Their passing is an inevitability, and at the same time it is filled with a feeling of loss and deep grieving because of the depth of love we share for them and our longing for their company, loyalty, innocence and unshakable faith in us, their human. Like Truffles, the beautiful boxer who graces the cover of this book, they become, in their short time with us, a beacon of light, a best friend and a pillar of strength. Their spirits will be forever remembered, loved and honoured within each of us and their light will not go out.

Thank you, furry, feathered and scaled ones. Our lives would not be remotely the same without you in them. You are a big part of what inspires our days, brightens our outlook and gives us hope for the future. Your presence transforms us—it inspires us to be kinder, more compassionate, loving people.

A huge thank you to our cover models, Cathy Hamilton and her dog, Truffles (Truffles is also on the back cover).

I have had the distinct pleasure of knowing Cathy as a friend and colleague, and witnessing first-hand the beautiful loving connection she and her husband, Neil, shared with their boxer, Truffles.

Truffles and Cathy were the stars of an amazing photo shoot with photographer Devon Gillott and me, a little under a year before Truffles passed away suddenly on April 20th, 2015 due to cardiomyopathy. She will be forever remembered for her perma-grin, her adorable butt wiggles, her unending love and positivity, and all the goodness she gave to this world. Thank you, Cathy and Neil, for allowing me to share her beautiful spirit with the world, and to Cathy for braving the cover to honour and remember her for a very long time to come. Rest in peace, gorgeous girl, and thank you.

More Gratitude

Thank you to my countless furry gurus: to my mare, Diva, who, as with everything, was a catalyst in writing this book; to my beautiful whippet, B, who lovingly shared with me the truth about passing over during our magical and miraculous final two years together; to my dog, Kia, and my cat, Parker, for their support on this project, and to all the animals who have shared their wisdom, understanding and unconditional love with me. Gratitude to Sheena Bull, Linda Joy, Dari Rank, my family and many many more for seeing and believing in me as an author. Deep appreciation to photographer and dear friend Devon Gillott for her stunning and powerful captures of the true essence of every being she works with. And a big, huge thank you to Celeste and Bradley Morris and Sasha the dog for your beautiful and essential contributions.

Introduction

Death sucks. Period. I have yet to meet an animal lover who feels differently. It is an inherently messy, emotional, uncomfortable and challenging time. But what if it could suck just a little less? What if, instead of sucking the life out of you, draining your joy, and causing you to feel like a ship without an anchor, the final transition of your animal could feel different, easier, and maybe even sacred? In North America, as in much of the world, navigating death is a bit of a mystery. There is no class in school, no perfect time to sit down as a family and discuss this much-avoided topic. In fact, I would hazard a guess that death is even more taboo a topic than money and sex. And yet, it is something that is bound to happen, an inevitability, and with animals, given their short life expectancies, it occurs with even more frequency. Death can suck, but I know from personal experience that it's even worse when combined with a lack of understanding and strategies for navigating it.

After working with hundreds of animals and their hu- mans as a wellness consultant and animal intuitive, spe- cifically around this inevitable final transition, I've learned a few things. First, death is always hardest on those who are left behind. It can be deeply challenging, emotionally charged and even traumatizing. Second, the biggest concern of our animals during this transition is often about us—their favourite human—and how we are coping with their passing. Animals seem to possess an innate understanding and acceptance of this transition that goes beyond logical understanding. And third, there is an opportunity here, in the dying process, for a huge amount of healing and growth for everyone involved.

I wish I could promise that this book will be all sunshine and rainbows and glitter farts, but alas, it will probably leave you a bit teary and requiring a tissue or two. This is not an easy subject to traverse—it can be a minefield of emotions and memories. I promise to lighten up this somber topic as much as I can, in attempt to move it more and more into the light of day so that we can actu- ally change the way that we navigate through its twists and turns.

To help me on this mission are my co-authors Celeste Morris and Bradley Morris, who will be sharing about the recent transition of their beautiful dog, Sasha, and their inspiring and moving journey through the process. And, without getting too "woo-woo" about it, I can promise that your beloved animal companions on the other side are loving that you're here, reading this, healing your hearts and remembering their beautiful spirits. I recommend some tissues, some delicious chocolate by your side, and regular breaks filled with yoga or beach walks or baths or _____ (insert something that makes you feel good here) as you embark.

Thank you for being here and taking this powerful journey with me—it takes a huge amount of courage and willingness.

I am high-fiving you through the airwaves!

xoxo

Alexa and the crew (Diva (below), Kia and Parker)

Chapter 1

So short a stay

Like many of you, I have been an animal lover since before I can remember. I was the kid with her bedroom walls completely plastered with horse posters and her bookshelves stuffed full of James Herriot and how-to horse books. When asked what I wanted to be when I grew up, I answered without hesitation "a veterinarian." I tortured my parents incessantly throughout my childhood and teenage years with "Mom, can I have a horse?" and "Dad, can I go horse-back riding?" Born into a dog family, as the oldest child, I literally began my days with a dog as my very hesitant best friend. Byron, a springer spaniel with an intense dislike for anything that got between him and his beloved people (namely my parents), put up with me begrudgingly. Looking back, I'm certain he knew that letting out his true feelings towards these constantly multiplying and horrifically noisy little ones would only lead to trouble. So instead he chose the role of caregiver.

My fascination with animals only grew as I aged. I gravitated towards animals naturally, picking up garter snakes and frogs, and "rescuing" and caring for any animal that would allow me to. I quickly took on the role of the family dog walker and would constantly imagine myself riding a horse as I walked/trotted to school, a habit I continue at 35 years of age.

My very first pet of my own was a grey and white hamster named Squeaky. He was, for all intents and purposes, my best friend (sorry Byron). Looking back, I am astonished that he survived our many hair-raising adventures unscathed. Only later did it dawn on me that perhaps he didn't enjoy bouncing on the trampoline, swimming in the sink, or joining me in my hoodie pocket for long and bumpy bike rides. This little fellow definitely had his fair share of adventures!

At the very ancient hamster age of five years, Squeaky passed on. This was my first experience of death and loss, and at the tender age of 10 years, I was inconsolable over the loss of my little friend. Having no training or understanding about death and dying, I didn't know why he had left and where he had gone. I had no idea what death was all about and how to deal with it. After all, this isn't something we learn about in school. Because my grieving did not feel understood and acceptable, I did it privately, locked in my room, feeling an incredible amount of pain, and yet feeling like my behaviour, my grief, was wrong in some way or too much.

After Squeaky's passing, I felt a disconnect occur somewhere deep within, a shutting down of sorts. It was as if my then open and vulnerable heart shut and locked the door. Afterwards, I felt unable to connect deeply to the other animals in my life, changing the very nature and foundation of my relationships with animals. I became more callous, even cold, armouring myself against future heartbreak and the subsequent feelings of grief and loss. A subconscious pattern had been created around death and dying that would affect me for many years to come.

Looking back now, I see that I had a deep fear of the pain and grief that I knew would come when my animals eventually passed on. My new, surprisingly effective strategy for dealing with the pain and grief of loss was to not connect or love deeply in the first place, limiting the depth and quality of my relationships with the animals in my life.

Now, many years later, my understanding of death and dying has completely changed, reflecting the transformation that has happened in my world and my perception over the last twelve years. To say that I see the world and death completely differently would be an understatement.

To explain what has changed in my understanding, we need to rewind to twelve years ago and the beginning of my foray into energy medicine and working with animals as a career. This was a time of unprecedented changes in my perspective as my then black-and-white world began turning to brilliant technicolour. It was also a turning point in understanding the essential role that animals play in teaching us about this challenging and inevitable transition—their short lifespans often forcing us to navigate the difficult twists and turns of death and dying of a loved one much more often than with our human family or friends.

I had recently graduated from the University of Victoria with a Bachelor of Science in Kinesiology, and had applied and been accepted to a school that would return me to my lifetime passion for horses. Little did I know that the learning path I was embarking on was rich with energy medicine and teachings in consciousness and self-awareness, subjects that, at the time, were the equivalent of learning to speak Japanese. I had no awareness, understanding or knowledge of these aspects whatsoever, a fact that was accompanied by an initial and pronounced resistance on my part to these new concepts.

My initial resistance to these new ideas and seemingly foreign perspective melted quickly into an insatiable thirst for understanding and a voracious appetite for learning. I had an un-traditional learning style that accompanied this process, complete with emotional outbursts, conflict, tantrums and the painful uncovering and healing of years and years of "stuff." By "stuff," I mean intense perfectionism and self-inflicted inner criticism, very poorly developed emotional intelligence, major fear of failure and rejection, and paralyzing doubt in my own skills and wisdom. I realized through this process that I was a highly sensitive, deeply feeling empath who had spent a lifetime attempting to be anything but.

My unprocessed and deeply buried stuff, and the journey through and beyond it, is now a big part of my path as an author, healer and teacher, informing my purpose and my passion. In fact, everything I share in the coming pages was learned through the rather intense process of fully understanding my experience, and through the journey into my personal lion's den of emotions, self-inflicted judgment and scrutiny. Feeling a teaching "in my bones" through experience, and trying a few different ways of being on for size, is the way I best come to understand a new way of thinking. Perhaps you too can relate to this sensation of deep knowing that can only come from "living it." Experience is, often, the most powerful teacher.

At Equine Therapy School, where my journey into energy medicine began, my primary teachers were head instructor Dave Collins and hundreds of horses. I was blessed to have every kind of horse from every walk of life in my teaching staff, including my own mare, Diva. Diva, my very first horse, chose me about two months into my adventure into Equine Sport Therapy. This is a story for another time, but suffice it to say that our connection is stronger than ever almost twelve years later and she continues to be one of my greatest teachers and my very best friend. She is also one of the reasons I am writing this book, because I know that losing her is going to be one of the most challenging experiences of my life, and I want to be able to move through this transition at her side, as her best friend, as gracefully as humanly possible. Yes, I did warn you that tissues would be a good thing.

All of the horses I worked with through my education as an Equine Sport Therapist were more than happy, even eager, to teach me what this energy medicine stuff was all about. Some of the lessons included how to trust my intuition, how to go with the flow, how to not take on other people's or animals' "stuff," how to understand what healing is really about, and how to let more joy and fun into my world. And, of course, they began to teach me about how animals experience and perceive death. What they shared—and continue to share—has completely shifted my own perception.

You see, animals have a very different view of death and dying than we do. In fact, their whole view of life itself is as inspiring as it is pragmatic. Over the coming chapters, we'll be exploring these unique viewpoints and how they can help us to more gracefully navigate all the transitions in our lives, and especially the inevitable transition that is death and dying.

As my skill, confidence and business grew, people began to ask for my help during their animal's final transition, a deeply challenging time for most animals and their people. While uncomfortable at first, I felt a growing gratitude for being trusted in what I was beginning to understand was a profound opportunity for connection and potential transformation. So much of this work was about helping owners and their animals move gracefully through this powerful and inevitable transition. Like a surfer on a wave, peace seemed to come with accepting the presence of the wave and, as gracefully as possible, riding it to its completion. But there was often "stuff" in the way, and this invariably created resistance to the inevitable and made the transition much more challenging for everyone concerned. I began to see how this "stuff" could be shifted and released through energy work and a shift in perspective, or how we perceive life, death, dying and connection as a whole (I'll dive more deeply into what I mean by this shortly). Over and over, I experienced how different this transition could be for people and their animals when the right support, tools and understanding were available.

One of the big take-aways from my decade of work with animals and their favourite people is this: our animals are more deeply connected to us—their people—than we could ever imagine. This connection is literally vast and endless in its complexity and in its love, and many of the threads of these connections are completely intangible and mysterious. As we'll begin to learn in the coming pages, this connection between animals and their owners is extremely powerful. It is one of the reasons why the death of our animals is so painful, at times bordering on excruciating. They are a deeply beloved and intricately connected member of our family. And they often serve many roles in our family matrix that we are not even aware of, roles that can leave painful gaps in our lives and in our hearts with their passing.

Amazing, sometimes miraculous, shifts often occurred during sessions with animals and their people, often during their final days, as we explored the deeper roles of the animals in our lives and unpacked our connections to them and our current understanding and perception of death and dying. Old and outdated beliefs and patterns around death and dying would change, and clients began trusting in their intuition to know when the timing was right to let go. Dogs would begin to gracefully step down from the jobs they had held their whole lives and finally let go into relaxation, and herds of horses would find peace in the death of a loved herd member. With each experience of this nature, my understanding deepened, my heart opened and my reverence grew. I began to see that death and dying was yet another area where we can find deeper understanding, love and compassion if we just know where to look.

One of the amazing benefits of practicing energy medicine is that through all these healing sessions done on others, I was also healing myself. How good is that? The same goes for when we do energy work for ourselves—everyone benefits. Many of the patterns I had held my whole life vanished, including much of my old "stuff" around connection, loss, and abandonment, and the high and seemingly indestructible walls I had constructed when my beloved hamster Squeaky passed on. Experiences that had previously been a trigger for me seemed to no longer hold an emotional charge, and the same was apparent in my animals and those around me. Perhaps most importantly, my heart felt healed and, in this important area, whole.

And it couldn't have been better timing; these shifts in my experience were put to the test not long after. When the extremely difficult time came three years ago to put my cat, Smoochie, a beautiful and sweet 16-year-old grey and white tuxedo, out of his physical pain, the choice was clear—I could see it in his eyes and feel it in my heart. My veterinarian confirmed my feeling after a thorough examination. Thankfully, my years of experience connecting with other animals helped me to feel sure that the timing was right. He was ready. As his body relaxed into his final transition, I felt what I had experienced with so many animals—a profound sense of peace and freedom, as he moved out of a restricted and uncomfortable physical body into a space of release. For him, death was nothing more than another transition, a re-calibrating of our relationship, not a disconnection or an ending, as I had previously believed. It was powerful to feel this truth with my own family member and, through this new understanding, be able to stay connected with his presence even though he was no longer with me physically. Yes, I deeply grieved not having this beautiful boy at my side physically, but the depth of connection remained unshaken.

Since then, I have always felt connected to him, which is a huge gift. My intuitive practices allow me to connect with his spirit whenever I need to. I think of him with a heart full of joy and gratitude for the time and experiences we had together. I meet the waves of grief and loss that come up with acceptance and love, knowing that they are a natural part of the process and of remembering, not something to fix or change.

Most noticeable and noteworthy though is this: I no longer fear connecting deeply and wholeheartedly with the animals who enter my life. I've been able to let go of the paralyzing fear that had been based on their short life span and the inevitability of navigating more final transitions at the side of my animals and experiencing the painful feelings of grief and loss in the process. I have instead, embraced my role as steward and guide of the unique and incredible animals that choose to travel with me for their short, yet powerful stint here on Earth.

Because of this transformation and my openness to connection, I now have another incredible cat in my life who I am deeply in love with—a black and white tuxedo named Parker, who in many ways reminds me of Smoochie! He's a daily blessing—full of energy and life, and hilariously rambunctious. Many of you will know the feeling of having animals who choose you and not the other way around; Parker definitely did the day he walked up to me with unparalleled conviction, his tail held confidently, as if to say, "What took you so long?" He was an eight-week-old kitten with the spirit and fearlessness of a tiger. I can say for sure that our connection has already, in two short years, provided me with remarkable insight, unrivaled hilarity and joy, and incredible inspiration. Much of this is due to my willingness to be vulnerable and connect, despite the inevitability of a drastic change in the nature of our connection at some point during our journey together.

Before my somewhat bumpy introduction to energy medicine over a decade ago, I would never have believed that we are capable of deep transformation in our way of being in the world. I believed, like so many of us do, that our patterns, perception and way of being in the world are set in stone, unaffected by any outside attempts to change them. I know now that each one of us is capable of opening these doors to a new perception of our world and our experiences in it. I am proof, as are the countless clients, friends and colleagues who have experienced deep and lasting shifts physically, mentally and emotionally in themselves and their animals, along with the millions worldwide who are engaged in work of this nature as we speak.

Animals, by their nature, are living proof of this possibility. The consciousness of most animals exemplifies where we can be and where peace and understanding lie. Even their grieving process outlines a potentially different and more healing path for us in the realm of death and dying—one that sucks way, way less than our current version. There seems to be an understanding in each species of how to honour, process and release their loved ones during their last rites. Typically it is done in a ritual unique to the group or species. For example, if you watch horses or elephants in the wild (and even, at times, in domestication), they will stay with and even protect the body of their fallen family member or herd mate for as long as necessary to complete their process of letting go. There is a reverence, a sacredness and definitely a spiritual understanding in their behaviour, as if they trust in a perfect timing and creating a sacred space for these potent rites to play out.

Developing the feeling, timing and conscious awareness that we observe in our animal companions requires patience, humility and a willingness to change, to be more open and honest than we ever thought possible. It is, by its nature, a rather uncomfortable process—our craving for familiarity and sameness destines it to be so. But the rewards are well worth the effort, as we begin to experience the flowing, even creative, process that is the last rite of passage, an essential and inevitable journey that each of us must witness and experience as a part of our experience on this fine, albeit challenging, planet we call Earth.

Chapter 2

Why death sucks so much

"We live in a culture where it has been rubbed into us in every conceivable way that to die is a terrible thing."
–Alan Watts

When I started thinking about something I would like to help animal lovers with, the subject of death and dying came to mind right away. Not only is it an area that has affected me to a great degree in my life and career, and something I feel a strong sense of connection to, it is also an experience that every animal lover has to face a time or two, or quite possibly more, during their lifetime. And saying goodbye to our animals is rarely easy or comfortable. In fact, as the title of this book clearly states, it can really suck.

I've seen firsthand how a different understanding of the transition of death and dying in our animals can, by tiny increments or great bounds, change this experience. How such a potentially tragic transition can transform into a sacred one full of connection and love. This lit a fire of inspiration within me. These flames were further fanned by the tragic stories of people suffering deeply and at length from the loss of a beloved animal friend and companion, sometimes even refusing to have another animal in attempt to prevent future heartbreak.

For many of us, even the word death itself is hard to say or think about. It holds its own energetic imprint, an energy that changes depending on our culture, beliefs and upbringing. For example, if I lived in a specific area of India, my experience of the word death would be very different due to my religious or spiritual understanding, my cultural imprinting and the behaviour I observed in my role models during times of dying and death, namely my family. In that culture, I may have been taught at an early age that people re-incarnate and that death is a transition that should be freely grieved as much as is necessary for each individual.

The combination of these factors and their effect on my perception has created a very different experience of death since my childhood reaction to Squeaky, my hamster, passing on. In our westernized culture, the subject of death is often taboo, and often not discussed or explained, so my 10-year-old self had no framework to understand what was happening. It is understandable, then, that many of us have what might be considered "over-reactions" to death and the dying process. Even my parents and teachers, as much as they wanted to help me, did not necessarily have a framework with which to help my 10-year-old self understand. Our discomfort with facing and "unpacking" our unique beliefs, patterns and current experience of death—feeling equally uncomfortable discussing and exploring this essential topic with others—is one of the big reasons why I knew I had to write this book, both for you and for me. After all, as animal lovers, we're never going to stop moving through the process of death and dying with our furry loved ones. And, if you are someone who loves animals, not allowing yourself to share your life with another animal as a way to prevent potential heartbreak just might suck even more than death itself.

Why death hurts so much

Alright, we're diving in. Why does the death of a loved one hurt so much? And is it even possible for it not to suck nearly as much? Remembering that in each one of us are entirely unique imprints around death, there seem to be a few common threads:

1) **Losing love is the worst.** Much of what we do as human beings—our motivation behind our actions and behaviours—is to prevent the loss of love. It is the reason we fear criticism, disapproval, rejection, abandonment and much more. Death, by its very nature, feels like the ultimate loss, with no potential for resolution, and no possibility of restoration of the love we once felt. It can feel like there is no turning back from this transition, and its finality feels deeply painful and terrifying on countless levels. The sense of loss that accompanies death cuts deep, tapping into seemingly endless wells of grief and, quite possibly, anger, guilt and fear as well. It is, on so many levels, the ultimate loss, with the entire physical landscape of our life irrevocably changed by the disappearance of a key player, and the love that they brought to our life.

2) **This grief is *all* our grief.** Like a giant fishing net, the death of our beloved furry companion and the feeling of grief accompanying this loss have the potential to bring up a heavy, overwhelming load of

16

unprocessed related emotions. The feeling that we're opening Pandora's box is very common, and with it comes the desire to stuff it all down, not look at it, and perhaps become distant toward any new animals entering our life or toward new experiences that might push our buttons and trigger an emotional on-slaught. The problem is this: the emotions are not go-ing anywhere. They stay in our body and do all sorts of not-so-fun things to our body and mind. Which is why, with the help of grief expert, Celeste Morris, we're later going to go deep into how to work with our own personal Pandora's box of emotions when they come up—an essential skill for all of us.

3) **We live in a physical world.** Or at least we tend to relate to it that way. Which means that when one of our animals no longer exists physically in it, we feel like the connection is gone forever. But is it true? That depends on the person and their perception. Because what is true for one may not be true for another. Here's the thing, though: our truth can change with experience and the integration of that experience. My truth back when I had my hamster, Squeaky, was that the world was purely physical. And that affected the way I perceived his death, creating a deeper sense of loss of love and connection. Now my truth is very, very different—I see the world as energy that mani-fests into tangible things. To me, everything is much more than just physical. And this truth allows me to stay connected with my animals long after they are

gone, because our connection doesn't depend on being together physically. I can let go into trusting that they are with me long after they have parted from their physical form. The result? Death, even though it is still a deep loss, a huge adjustment and an inherently challenging transition, has become something very different from my early experience of it.

4) **Death brings up questions about our own mortality.** Every time we experience death, it pushes on some major buttons relating to our very existence and our own mortality. And that can really suck. No one enjoys pondering their own death and what that will mean, partly because it opens the door to a million other questions and concerns around what happens after, heaven and hell, who and what we're leaving behind, and what kind of mark we have left on the world. This is one of those doors that most of us, understandably, choose to keep under lock and key. It is definitely not all sunshine and unicorns back there. But keeping this door locked might just suck more than hauling it open and courageously looking at what lies behind it. Because as long as that door is under lock and key, as long as we continue to deny that death is a reality we are eventually going to have to face, we are not fully living and we are never fully present in our lives. And that definitely sucks.

5) **The death of our animals is often downplayed by our society.** If you are an animal lover, you have more than likely lost at least one, if not many, beloved furry family members. Each passing feels different, but none is void of loss or grief. And yet, we live in a society that has, historically, downplayed our experience of loss and the potency of our grief. We hear comments like "It's just a dog" or "Why are you so upset?" and they make our stomachs churn and steam come out of our ears. For many of us, myself included, we may feel closer to our animals than to anyone else in our lives. We trust them with our hearts, we love them with a depth and strength that is hard to describe, and we come to rely on their love, connection and presence to move us through our days. Is it any wonder that their passing from this world can bring deep despair and feelings of unbearable loss? Add to this the experience of guilt and shame for feeling so deeply and you've got the makings of something incredibly sucky. Let's unpack this area a little further, shall we?

"It's just a _____..."

I don't think I'm the only one who has heard this one comment and felt ripped apart, completely confused and questioning the entirety of my inner knowing. Because inside, we know that this is so much more than just a dog, or a horse, or a cat, or a hamster. We know that this is our best friend, our confidant, our teacher, and, in many cases, our saviour. Our furry four-legged besties have been there for us through the thickest and the thinnest, sticking by our side when others may not have had the guts or the compassion, carrying us through our moments of "What's the point?" and all the times we held onto our life and our world by a thread. They are what makes it all worth it.

We all have come from lineages and countless generations who believed "it's just a dog," generations that downplayed and coldly detached from the perceived and played-out inequality of animals. Our relatives lived in very different times and had very different ways of thinking, especially when it came to animals and their treatment. Just a few generations ago, the world was at war and connecting with or even caring about animals was probably the last of most people's worries. They had to survive and their relationships with animals were more than likely solely based on that necessity. Animals were often perceived as non-emotional, unintelligent sources of food, work and resources.

Now, thankfully, all of that is changing quickly, and for the better. Animals are, more and more often, being seen as they truly are—equals, trusted guides, beloved members of our families, and teachers. With each generation, the depth of our love, appreciation and understanding of our animals grows and with it, the strength of our connection. Is it any wonder that the final transition of our animals affects us so much more deeply and profoundly than it might have affected our ancestors, and that our sense of loss equals the grief we feel when we lose a beloved family member? Because the reality is, that is the truth of what has occurred.

Through all of this sharing, my main point is this: our animals are not just animals, just as you are not just a human being. They are multi-faceted and much loved members of our tribe, they are equals and teachers, they hold an essential place in our hearts, and they are missed after their passing every bit as much, if not more, than the people in our lives. On that note, I give you full permission to give the stink eye to anyone who has the audacity to tell you "it's just a dog." You don't need that kind of negativity in your life. And I'm only half-kidding, because you really really don't.

The middle road

My personal experience has shown me that there are two main ways we handle death and dying in North American culture. I have tried on both of these coping strategies personally and encountered them countless times in my work. What they lack in efficacy, they make up for in sheer volume of use - from very small children these two strategies were modeled to us as appropriate ways to process, or, more accurately, not process, death and dying.

The first strategy, and the lesser used of the two, is to become emotionally turbulent, overwhelmed, incapable and inconsolable, with our Pandora's box of emotions staying open and raw in perpetuity. Our sense of loss becomes like a festering wound, never really healing in a healthy way. We often feel incapable of moving forward in a healthy way, leading us to shut the door to other animals or opportunities to enter our lives, in the hopes of "stopping the bleed."

The second strategy is to become closed and even callous, unable to get in touch with the uncomfortable emotions that are bound and determined to rise to the surface. We stop breathing fully, feeling deeply or connecting to what could, potentially, hurt us. Essentially, we go numb. We might refer to this as bottling up or stuffing our emotions. This was my chosen coping strategy when my first hamster, Squeaky, passed on, after strategy number one failed miserably.

Both of these strategies can seem effective in their own way, potentially preventing further heartbreak and hurt, but both have a deeply detrimental catch. You see, both of these strategies stop us from really "being" with our beloved animal in their final time with us and throughout their lives, just as they stop us from experiencing the potent, heart-opening and connecting nature of this sacred transition. Our relationships with our animals take on a hollowness and a sense of distance, designed by the mind to keep us safe from further emotional harm. We may even forgo welcoming another animal into our life and all the joy that could bring, or connecting meaningfully and wholeheartedly with our current animals out of fear of further hurt and heartbreak. And in both cases, our experience of our animal's death is one that often fails to create a sense of resolution and growth, leaving us scarred and scared for many years to come—a stark contrast to the unprecedented healing that is possible for all involved with a slight change in our approach.

When I think about the cost, merely on a personal level, of not knowing how to move gracefully through the inevitable process of death and dying, it becomes even clearer how important it is to talk about. Even as a young child, the cost for me was huge—not having the deep connections with animals that were really possible, and feeling escalating fear and confusion around death, loss and abandonment. Employing these disconnecting and disempowering strategies also affected my other relationships, causing me to shut down emotionally, bottle my emotions (much to the detriment of my body and mind), and retreat into myself for solace rather than seeking help and support from loved ones. And like so many of the animal lovers I've worked with, I felt guilty for not being able to help more, and for not being able to keep Squeaky alive. I even found myself believing that his death was my fault in some way, feeling the unbearable weight, for one of the first times in my short life, of shame and guilt.

The more I talked with my clients about the personal costs of not feeling able to handle death and everything it involves, the more it was evident that we pay a price in more areas than just our emotional state. One friend shared her experience of paying over $10,000 in fees on a storage locker containing her deceased father's belongings. Because she was unable to enter the locker after his passing without breaking down, it took her years to build up the courage to go in and let go, both physically and emotionally. I have also heard many stories of people deciding to never get an animal again, cutting themselves off from years of fun and companionship because their pain and fear of losing another animal was so great. Others relay the guilt they feel around their decision to put their suffering animal down, or around a decision they feel may have shortened their lifespan or, alternatively, created suffering. This is a burden they carry around daily that affects their sense of self and worth, and their trust in themselves as a steward of other animals.

It's clear that death and dying is an aspect of pet stewardship and life that can be a huge minefield of unprocessed grief, fear, guilt and confusion. As a practitioner who works specifically with this issue, I have seen firsthand the damage that can be done if we don't find support and healing when we need it. But because it's so difficult to talk about, asking for help and guidance can feel like a very large and very vulnerable stretch.

So how do we find resolution, support and healing within this touchy and very uncomfortable, yet inevitable, area of life? I coined the term "the D-word" a while back to denote how little our society likes to talk about death and dying. Even trying to say the word death out loud in the comfort of our own home can be challenging. It feels like a "bad" word, sometimes even a bad omen. And yet, it is an experience that every one of us has to face numerous times during our lives and that we will have to navigate ourselves. Death is, at its essence, inevitable. Before you get choked and close this book on me for being such a downer, hear me out.

You may have noticed by now that we are taught on countless occasions as children what to pay attention to and, more importantly, what to avoid. Don't look at that, don't think about this, don't be that, don't do that. We often grow up with a strong belief that when something is uncomfortable (which death definitely is), it needs to be fixed, ignored or denied. Because death is not something we can "fix," although many have tried their darnedest, we typically turn to our other two options: ignoring it and denying it.

As a child, suppression and denial can be very helpful skills and are often vitally important in keeping us safe and comfortable. But as we get older, the earlier helpful effects start to wear off, eventually leaving us with a weighty and emotionally charged burden of un-dealt-with "stuff." We end up carrying this exhausting and cumbersome weight, believing it is our burden to bear with no resolution or release possible. We start to wonder why we hurt so much, why life feels just OK, or we just don't experience the vitality or happiness that we used to.

Then there is the inevitable moment when it all starts pouring out, usually precipitated by a triggering event or experience. We begin losing our cool, crying at every sad commercial, flying into a rage, and feeling low energy, uninspired and incapable. We may even experience illness or pain. And because we don't know how to deal with the incredible onslaught of emotion coming up, we attempt to find new ways to control it and ignore it. Enter addictions of all sorts (my go-to's are Netflix and peanut-butter-chocolate anything) and other weird and not-so-wonderful coping strategies. Sound familiar?

Like a bucket that has finally filled to the brim, now spilling uncontrollably over the edge, our mind and body can no longer contain all of the pent-up emotion. When years of pent-up emotions begin to spill over the top, we are frequently surprised and confused by the onslaught. The reality is that our issue began when the very first drop fell in the bucket, and built up slowly over time until the inevitable moment when we start to fall apart. At some point, we have to allow what is inside to come out, as scary as that prospect may seem.

The stark and hard-to-swallow reality is this: denial of death only leads, ironically, to a distinct lack of life. We become, by necessity, numb. But what if we could stop this process before we get to that point? Or if we do, what if we could learn how to live without denial or suppression, or fear that our Pandora's box of emotions will never ever end, and instead, in full, healthy expression? Read on, my friend. Your path to this very real possibility lies ahead. But first, let's talk about avoidance.

When we avoid something, nothing about it actually changes. The world continues to turn and the experience we are avoiding continues to happen, regardless of whether we choose to be a part of it or not. This is both really annoying and really awesome. When we talk about being conscious, what it really means is exposing these scary places and really looking at the things we least want to look at. When we can look at these places, we can start to heal them, just as with the monster under the bed when we were kids. These childhood monsters weirdly just got larger and scarier the more we avoided them, and magically disappeared when we finally worked up the courage to peek our head down there and take a look.

This is why the death and dying process is so natural for certain cultures—especially for our animals. Denial and suppression are not a part of their experience, which allows the full expression of their feelings as they naturally want to happen. Through this one key shift, the process of death and dying changes from a heady, logical process to a sacred one full of feeling and reverence.

The irony is that trying to deal with death on a solely logical level never seems to end, due to unprocessed experiences and the crazy-making head games that tend to tag along, while the sacred, feeling-based experience of death and dying moves gracefully to a point of natural conclusion and resolution. The completed state includes honouring and lovingly remembering the parted, feeling connected to them on another, less tangible level, riding the waves of grief that arise as a natural part of this process, and allowing their lives and all the incredible ways they have touched us to permeate our present and future. Although the feeling-based experience definitely involves more discomfort in the short-term as we courageously look our fears in the eye and traverse the waves of emotion that are naturally arising, the long-term benefits are pretty awesome.

A shift in perspective

One of the most amazing things about being human is our ability to shift and change, not only our behaviour and our thoughts, but the entire way we experience the world. The very act of making such a shift, however, takes tremendous courage. We are working against generations of programming that reiterate time and time again that sameness is safe and the way we have always done life and death is how we should continue. We are programmed, deep down in our reptilian brains, to seek out familiarity, even if the familiar lost its usefulness long ago. Don't worry. The next few chapters will help you to step out of this old programming in a way that feels safe and entirely possible. From this new and less cramped vantage point, you just might be able to see the world from a whole new perspective.

Why is perspective so important? Because how you see something is different from how anyone else in the entire world sees that same thing. Even something as simple as an apple sitting on a plain table can be described in a million different ways, based on each person's unique life filled with unique experiences. When talking about death and dying, the same rings true. How you "see" death and dying is unique to your own experiences and understanding. We each have a lens, formed from our unique beliefs, fears, past experiences and cultural conditioning, that colours our view of our world and what we experience in it. So, an essential key to changing our relationship with death is in shifting the way we "see" things, or our perspective. This is a very simple process, although it's not easy; it can be summed up in two words: be willing.

Here's what I mean by that. Be willing to see things in a different way, be willing to be fully honest about how you currently see things, and be willing to have a new experience around death and dying. I like to imagine this process as opening a door to a new possibility, a door that might feel scary and unfamiliar, but nonetheless holds behind it what you're needing to change your perspective and, therefore, your experience. In the process, you will notice a shift in every area of your life, as your shift in how you see the world ripples out into all areas of your day-to-day experience. Willingness implies openness, a state that is necessary if healing is to occur in any area of our lives.

If you are willing, let's get to work and begin to explore how we experience our reality. How present are you? What does emotion mean to you? What is your truth? What do you believe? How do you perceive your world? And finally, what is death all about, really?

Chapter 3

The real deal

You might have heard me pop the word "presence" into our conversation a few times now. Yes, subliminal messaging is fun and all, but shall we bring this conversation out into the open already? Because it's an important one, especially when it comes to our furry loved ones. Presence is essential for our animals, and there is a distinct and important reason for this. Let's define "being present" as the state when our minds and bodies are hanging out in the present moment, rather than in the past or the future. It's the state that animals are in most of the time.

Yep, animals live in the present moment pretty much all the time—it's just one part of what makes them so awesome. They don't think of the future with trepidation, or stress and worry over the past. Their minds, for the most part, are firmly planted in the here and now. But if we look at human thought process and the nature of the mind, for example yours, what percentage of your time do you spend in the here and now? We're all about honesty here, so just think of a rough daily estimate. Don't worry, no judgment here—if your answer was in the low percentages, you're not alone, in fact, you're in the norm. I would hazard a guess that the majority of us in North America hang out in the present moment for about 30 minutes per day, if that. In other cultures where meditation is a way of life, this number is likely quite a bit higher. Before I entered Equine Sport Therapy School and the teaching ground of horses, I was rarely, if ever, in the present moment. It was an issue, but somehow I got away with it for almost 23 years without too much uproar. Horses, however, have a way of insisting that you be right here, right now. Disconnected, distracted humans are actually a major liability in their eyes. In fact, my mare, Diva, will often step on my feet as a way of reminding me to reconnect (at present I am nursing a rather fabulous bruise from just such a reminder).

My first experience indicating how far from the present moment I was actually living was in my inaugural month of practical work at the BC College of Equine Therapy. The program I was taking was set up so that the majority of our time was spent at home working with horses. That first month was excruciating for me. Why? The horses I had planned to work with would not let me anywhere near them. My only task was to massage a few recently discovered muscles in their necks and I couldn't even get close to a neck to try! When I went back to school, certain that I had made a terrible decision applying in the first place, my teacher, Dave, took me aside and said gently, "Alexa, I think it's time we teach you how to ground."

Grounding is a process to enhance the experience of being in the present moment by connecting your feet and body energetically to the earth, just as a tree grows roots to create connection. Dave explained that my ungrounded and disconnected energy was causing the horses I was trying to work with to feel unsafe in my presence and therefore move away from me. He also shared in the kindest way possible that my electromagnetic field, the unique energy field that surrounds each living being, was shooting energy everywhere, much like a plug in a wall that can be volatile and even dangerous without proper grounding. By picturing strong roots growing out of my feet, I was able to feel more relaxed and present in my body—and in my life in general. After that powerful lesson on being present, my horse "guinea pigs" were more than happy to let me work with them and no longer had a fear of being electrocuted.

Now, whenever an animal is upset or agitated around me and I can't find a source, I take a quick minute to get present and grounded, and very shortly after, they begin to relax. Essentially, I become their grounding prong, allowing them to release excess energy and feel more fully in their skin. This has a great side-effect of leaving me feeling very peaceful, akin to having a strong foundation supporting me, both physically and energetically.

(Listen to my favourite grounding visualization here: http://bit.ly/groundingvisualization.)

So, let's bring things full circle. How does being present and grounded help us during times of transition, especially challenging ones? When we become more available and connected to the present moment, several things shift in how we experience transition. First, we begin to relax about it. There is a big difference between approaching a transition, particularly our pet's final transition, from a state of being present, as opposed to thinking of every possible worst-case scenario and allowing our perception to be coloured by all the awful things that have happened in the past or could potentially happen in the future. I don't need to tell you that humans have fantastic imaginations, especially when it comes to creating and visualizing terrible, worst-case scenarios.

Fascinatingly, when we do dream up these scenarios and imagine them playing out in our life, we are creating the identical physiological response in our body that would occur if the worst thing ever did actually happen, complete with the accompanying hormonal changes, change in heart rate and spike in tension and adrenaline levels. It's interesting to note that athletes who visualize playing their sport in their minds experience similar if not the same physiological benefits as if they were actually playing.

In fact, astonishing as it may seem at first, our mind can't really tell the difference between what is real and what we are imagining. This can be both a blessing and a curse, especially when it comes to worst-case scenarios. The chances of the worst situation happening are, thankfully, low, but the tension and stress we create around that tiny little possibility can be huge. In essence, we can easily make ourselves a tad crazy. Translation? When we are frantic and in a self-imposed tailspin, it can be much more difficult to connect and communicate with our animals during their final time with us.

When we are living fully in the present moment, we get to engage our senses, feel more deeply and connect more strongly to what is really happening in each moment, and to our animal. We are also way more connected to our subtle senses, the senses that allow us to cultivate our ability to actually communicate with our animals—and not just through body language, although that's part of it.

Yes, it's true, our animals are giving us a great deal of information throughout our days together, connecting with us all the time through images, words and more. Being present hones our ability to hear what they are "saying" and has the potential to take our relationships with our animals to a whole new, very cool level. You can imagine how helpful this intuitive connection can be when navigating the timing and logistics of an animal's final transition.

Over the years, during intuitive sessions, many animals have shared their chosen timing, their preferred veterinarian, their last wishes, and their deep and ever-lasting love for their people, complete with pictures of their favourite experiences, and details on how they would like to be remembered. One German Sheppard shared that she would like to have a plaque made with her picture and a short poem to put above the barn to honour her years of service and love. This honouring process allowed her family to find resolution and to stay connected to her memory. Staying present also allows us to receive the support we need, which often arrives in weird and wonderful ways, to be open to emotions as they arise and move, and to share our love and stay connected even in a time of struggle. In essence, staying in the present moment allows a sucky situation to become far less sucky for everyone involved.

Comfortable with discomfort

As we practice staying in the present moment, we begin to realize that every transition is just a series of moments, nothing more and nothing less. Some of these moments might be exponentially more uncomfortable than the rest. We might want to resist those particular moments with everything we've got. That's OK and it is completely normal. Just notice how you feel and what you want to do. More than likely, a big part of you wants to escape the discomfort of the uncomfortable moments, dropping into some version of flight or fight as the body shouts at us to get out of this feeling in a hurry. In those moments, try to remember that we're all human and we never had a class in school on how to stick out the deeply uncomfortable and emotional moments. Most of us would rather climb Mt. Everest than face some of those.

I promise, once we cultivate the skills to navigate these experiences effectively, the understandable resistance towards emotionally charged moments will start to shift. The more we are able to "stay with" those icky, tricky moments (a skill we'll be developing over the next few chapters), the more our body and mind will realize that it's safe there even in the discomfort.

Remember, safety and comfort are the top two priorities of our body and mind. Understanding this one thing will shed light on much of our experiences, and our reactions to our experiences, up until this point. When we look at the initial motivation that created all of our patterns and coping mechanisms, we can see they were driven by the need or desire for one of these two things. So, it goes against the very grain of these patterns to "be" in discomfort and just stay there. It takes not only courage, and willingness, but also the right tools.

You better believe that the survival parts of your brain will be shocked initially by this new way of being, urging us to fight or flee the uncomfortable or "dangerous" situation. Dangerous is in quotation marks to denote that most situations perceived as dangerous by the mind are actually not dangerous at all when looked at from an aware and conscious place. Many of us have been taught that being "emotional" or feeling emotions that are perceived as negative, such as grief or anger, is not acceptable or normal, and therefore dangerous.

Quite the opposite is true—the processing and integrating of naturally arising emotions creates growth, awareness and much more actual safety. If we watch our animals, we see that they are masters at experiencing, processing and integrating in the moment, skills they have developed to cultivate awareness, harmony, physical and emotional safety, and well-being. This is a skill set that we're about to learn, and is essential to moving through our life's many transitions as gracefully as humanly possible.

In breath we trust

I've been alluding to a few essential skills for a while now and we're about to discover one of the most powerful. And it's so simple it's annoying. It's the breath. Seriously. The breath is critical when it comes to the cultivation of presence. In fact, if we look at most meditation traditions, the breath is at the centre of the practice. There are a number of reasons for this and I promise I'll get to them right away. But first, let's take a little inventory.

Sit up. Nice tall spine. And take a breath. What happens? Does your breath go high into your shoulders, lifting them up? Does it go down into your belly? Does it travel to the front of you? Or the back of you? To both sides of you or just one? Does it feel restricted or full? Take another breath, this time encouraging your in-breath to fill up your rib cage and belly and extend your spine. Then take another breath and then five more. With each breath, pay attention to where it's traveling, whether your breath meets resistance and what your breath moves in your body. Yes, you might just be a little light-headed right now. That's totally normal. We humans, we don't always breathe so well, so repetitive deep breaths can cause a noticeable rush of oxygen to the brain.

Now, take a minute to check in on how you're feeling. What do you notice about your mind? Is it in the future or in the past? Or is it in the present? The breath and our awareness of it has a wonderful way of keeping us firmly planted in the present moment, no matter what is happening in our world. And now, take a moment to check in with your body. What do you notice? How does it feel? What do you notice about your tension levels? Breathing is powerful medicine for cultivating relaxation in the body, allowing the tissues to unwind.

Using the breath as a tool to help us stay present with our experience, no matter how uncomfortable, allows the mind to start laying down new neural patterns that are reflective of our newfound relaxation and peace of mind. This is particularly true in those "uncomfortable" moments often found in transitions. Cool right? So, just the mere act of "staying with" our discomfort by focusing on the quality of our breath is enough to rewire the brain, change the very chemistry of our body and create wonderful ripples throughout our whole experience. Next time you've got a worst-case scenario on your mind, or can't stop thinking of that time when that awful thing happened, ask yourself what a golden retriever would do and take a deep breath, and then another, and then another (I dare you to add a little bum wiggle in for good measure and maybe a hug or two!).

The present moment yields incredible rewards and wonders, as we've started to experience. Ever wondered why it is so tough to remain there?

Why staying is harder...

I'm going to let you in on a little, but essential, secret about human beings and why it is so darn hard to stay present. I've learned this from years of my own self-discovery work and helping others move through their "stuff." Not only do parts of us love familiarity, but those very same parts also love to hold onto stuff! By stuff, I'm not just talking physical stuff, like that trophy you won in a baseball tournament when you were five and still have in a box in the basement. And yes, I still have that box and it's also filled with tiny animal figures from my dentist visits as a kid and papers from my grade three art class, and I'm sure it will all come in very handy one day! Sarcasm aside, we all tend to hang on to things are no longer relevant or helpful, with the idea that we might just need it one day.

Besides the stuff in our attics, I'm also referring to the emotional "stuff" that each of us carries around with us daily. These are the grudges, the resentment, the anger at a first boyfriend or father, the grief felt when your baby blanket finally got taken to the dump, the despair and hopelessness of losing a first pet. All of this stuff is hanging out in us all of the time and it can feel really, really heavy, like a chain around the ankle. That is, until the moment when we decide it's time to clean the house, or when the "house" makes that choice for us, which is always the more annoying of the two options.

Human beings are amazing at holding on. If our bodies and minds were basements, they would be stuffed to the ceiling full of belongings that we are never going to use again, but that we are quite certain we might need someday. If we picture an iceberg, much of what we are holding on to is stored in the part that is under the water. One of the reasons we hold on to all of this no-longer-useful stuff is that we are unaware that it is there, just as we are unaware of the sheer size of the base of the iceberg hiding under the water. This impressive ability to store information that is completely unconscious is the way that the subconscious mind works. It does this both to protect us and to store impressive volumes of information that it deems unimportant at this moment, and therefore not requiring conscious attention. This information, when triggered, informs our actions and reactions, our patterns of behaviour, and how we handle the twists and turns of life.

Everything we are holding on to in the unconscious is affecting our thoughts, actions and experiences and making it difficult to stay present, especially when our present experience includes something that triggers this tricky part of our mind. A trigger is essentially any event, person or situation that cues the subconscious mind to retrieve related, often emotionally charged information and, depending on the nature of the trigger, can cue the stress centres to react to potential danger or threats. In fact, every one of our past traumas, even those from fetal life and childhood, are stored away in the subconscious mind and can be potentially triggered by seemingly random events and situations. This fact alone is both fascinating and annoying all at once.

It makes sense, then, that instead of staying planted in the present moment, we are unceremoniously pulled this way and that by our attachments to the past, our trepidation about the future, our unprocessed and potentially traumatic experiences, and our outdated patterns of behaviour that were usually developed early in life. Most of our *modus operandi* for living life is laid down between fetal life and age 6, which is a fairly wild thing to think about. I don't know about you, but it's a little unnerving to think that much of my behaviour and actions in the world have their basis in patterns I laid down in my brain as a toddler. And yes, I still occasionally have a temper tantrum, although now, thankfully, they are much more of an internal affair.

The other big reason we hang on, getting pulled out of present moment, is that it lets us stay attached to our stories. And we all have stories. Stories like "my life is painful" and "it's all my fault" and "this person is terrible" and "that experience broke my heart and I'll never repeat it." Stories are vitally important to the human experience—as a way to share our journey and to understand, just a little, what has occurred. Storytelling is a lost and essential art. And each one of us has certain stories that could use a re-write.

As much as we might believe they help us or create our identity, these particular stories, the ones that paint us as a victim or keep us trapped in a never-ending cycle of limitation, actually can keep us locked in a life of longing, resentment and fear. Like trying to dance with a ball and chain around your ankle, the limiting stories we are holding on to about our life and ourselves affect our ability to transition gracefully and move forward easily in our life. So what do we need to do about it?

The trick here lies in two things. The first is to acknowledge the truth and the non-truth in your story, as limiting as it has been or has become. My story about my hamster, Squeaky, passing away went a little like this: When I was ten, my best friend left me alone and I had no idea where he had gone or how to bring him back. I felt lost and alone and devastated by this loss. I cried for days, my heart was broken, perhaps never to be repaired. I vowed to never let someone close enough to hurt me that badly again.

In this story, there is truth and there is non-truth. How I felt at the time was true—I was devastated and felt deeply lost and alone, not understanding or knowing how to move forward. It was an important and healing part of my story to acknowledge and accept the emotions I was feeling. Truthfully, missing this part of the story would be like leaving out the messy middle section of a book, or cutting the centre out of a painting—we would lose the wholeness of the experience. So often, because this middle bit is also the messy, emotional and uncomfortable bit, we try to skip a step and just "get on with things." The truth is, we can never skip out on this part—it is the part of the story that re-affirms that we are feeling, living, loving beings and not just robots, and it is the part that allows us to develop trust in our own capabilities and our limitless capacity for healing, compassion, depth and love.

What was not true about the story was this: I was not left alone or rejected by Squeaky, and even though my heart felt broken by this loss, it was capable of both repairing and being even more capable of great love. I, thankfully, broke my own vow, allowing myself to become even closer to other animals and people in my life, despite the fear of potential pain or hurt. These untruths, as you may even be able to feel, created limitation in my experience until I chose to let them go fully, which leads us beautifully to the second important step to moving forward easily.

Letting go. Because one of the tricks to all of this is to get just as amazing at letting go as we are at holding on. As the stewards of our animals, we need to become masters at letting go, true Jedis in the art of releasing what is no longer serving us. Once we've acknowledged, accepted and felt the truth and all the emotions and pain associated with it, there are three main things that we can do to help the process of releasing what is no longer serving us.

The first thing is to be willing and committed to transform the way we hold on and the way we let go. We need to uncurl our fingers from what we feel defines us and fully let go—not always an easy task. The second is something we've already talked about and we'll be talking about more: breathing. The breath is all about developing our ability to let go gracefully. The third is to accept, own and honour our own process of experiencing, integrating and releasing emotion, specifically grief.

Now, if these three things sound too simple to be true, remember that simple is not necessarily easy. Being willing and committed might look like a lot of things, including letting go of the need to be right, being loving and deeply compassionate with ourselves and others, even when we'd much rather do the exact opposite, and releasing our age-old excuses for not doing something that scares us. Willing might look like finally letting go of that grudge we've held since fifth grade, or letting the painful grief about a lost pet at age seven rise up to be felt and released. It might look like crying for days on end as a seemingly endless well of unprocessed emotion moves through our body. It might even look like moving through the anger at our parents for selling a childhood pony, filling journal page upon journal page with expletives, resentment and blame until we finally catch sight of a light at the end of the tunnel that looks and feels like love, acceptance and understanding. And it might definitely look like asking for help and support to do all of these things.

Being willing looks a whole lot like an equal combination of courage, humility and vulnerability, with the end result being freedom, release and spaciousness. We're going to get into how to let go of all of the stories and the stuff in just a second, but first, I want to dive a little deeper into the power of the breath.

Take a minute now to start becoming more conscious of your breath. Just as we did before, take several breaths into your rib cage and deep into your belly, then take a few more. When we become stressed, the first thing we lose is our deep relaxing breath, often in favour of a shallow, quick and relatively ineffective breath. And yes, there is a reason for this, which I'll get into in a moment. The irony, though, is that this deep and conscious breath is actually the key to allowing us to remain present and balanced in any stressful situation.

Our goal here is to help re-train your body and mind to continue to breathe consciously, even during potentially stressful experiences or transitions. The new neural pathways that will be laid down in your brain by making this simple, yet vital change will profoundly shift the way your system handles stress. This, in turn, will affect your perception, or the way you see the world, allowing the process of letting go to become more and more natural and easy.

Here are just a few essential reasons why engaging in conscious breathing can positively change our perception of our world and our experiences in it:

1. Our breath creates a powerful connection to our subconscious mind.

This part of the mind is completely unconscious, operating under the surface of our experience and colouring how we perceive and experience our world. We can permanently shift deeply ingrained patterns stored in the subconscious by focusing on taking deep, relaxing breaths into our belly during challenging times of stress and/or transition. Ironically, this is actually one of the reasons why we tend to avoid full breaths on these occasions—engaging in a healthy, full breath means that we also have to feel what's coming up, which is not always a pleasant sensation. By taking ineffective and shallow breaths, we are, in essence, attempting to avoid the messy "stuff."

Unfortunately, this age-old strategy only works for a limited time before the cap blows off of our well-sealed bottle of unprocessed emotion due to some seemingly unrelated event or situation. Often, when we are reacting to an experience, this reaction is being amplified by old patterns and experiences that are being triggered in the subconscious mind, somewhat similar to the metaphor of stepping unknowingly onto a minefield. These deep, unconscious patterns create our emotional and physical reactions to stressors and can keep us stuck in out-dated ways of thinking and responding. If we are able to understand our over-reaction as a natural part of this old "stuff" being agitated, then we can use the breath as a tool to let go of anything that is being triggered, even the really big stuff.

2. Our breath helps to keep us healthy.

Within our body and mind, the breath operates similarly to an X-ray machine, gathering information throughout the inspiration and expiration. The amount of information gathered is directly related to the depth of the breath. When it comes to letting go, a person with a strong, full and conscious inspiration and expiration in their breath will naturally and easily release blocks, unprocessed emotions and limiting patterns. Utilizing and understanding this built-in monitoring system is an amazing way to enhance the well-being of your body naturally. Not only that, but when we're breathing deeply, we are much more relaxed and all the tension that has been building up in our system can release.

3. Our breath keeps things flowing in our body and mind.

The breath can be a powerful force for movement and flow in the body. Through the movement of the body's four diaphragms, the breath massages the internal organs, encourages blood flow and enhances the function of the lymphatic system, our body's equivalent of a sewage system. Without this healthy flow, we can experience stagnancy in the body and mind, making it difficult to move forward freely on all levels. One constant I have found in my work is this: how the inner systems are working is directly reflective of the functioning of the outer systems (our relationship to our environment) and vice versa. Translation? If we want to flow on the outside, we need to flow on the inside.

4. Our breath helps us to easily process and work with stress and emotions.

The main diaphragm, a large flat muscle located directly under the ribs, not only helps us to breathe deeply but also doubles as an emotional processor and synthesizer. I often think of the diaphragm as the body's emotional garburator, processing our emotions as they arise from our moment-to-moment experience. This process is essential in distilling the wisdom and deeper understanding from our experiences, as challenging as those experiences might be.

When our emotions stay stuck in the diaphragm, it's the equivalent of putting piles of leftover food into the sink without ever turning the garburator on. Yep, it all gets rather messy and hard to deal with. Fortunately, the on-button is easy to find. All you have to do is remember to breathe with the intention of allowing your emotions to process, integrate and release—and the deeper the better.

5. Our breath helps to keep us in the present moment and in the flow of letting go.

It is difficult to breathe deeply, fully and consciously and worry about the past or future. Seriously, breathing with awareness takes major concentration. In order to breathe with awareness, we need to pay attention or we'll soon find our breath has become quick and shallow or has disappeared entirely. This is one reason why many meditation and yoga practices engage the breath as a focusing tool.

Our expiration relates to our ability to let go of the old carbon dioxide, creating space for the new rejuvenating and life-giving oxygen. This is reflective of our ability to let go of the old "stuff" stored away in our body and minds, and make space for something different and way more supportive! Using the breath consciously in this manner can be powerful for clearing out blocks to your innate well-being and your ability to move through difficult times gracefully. Practising with your animal present can be particularly helpful, as they will actually mirror or copy your breath. The term that is used to describe this incredible phenomenon is the syncopated breath, and can be both a blessing and a curse, depending on your level of awareness. If you notice your animal becoming agitated around you, check your breath to be sure it is slow and deep. For an older or imbalanced animal, syncopating your breath can be a great way to improve life for both of you, giving you both more energy and greater peace of mind. Nothing like a little massage from your diaphragm to wake up the whole system and create flow and ease!

Breathing 101

In many healing modalities, breathing is the heart of the practice. Really it is no wonder, as the breath is capable of bringing the body-mind into a full awareness of itself, or if the breath is not full, it can have all sorts of interesting and not-so-desirable effects. Many of us breathe shallowly, often just into our chest area, failing to fully utilize the incredible volume of our lungs. A full breath can be felt throughout the body, causing substantial movement in the diaphragm and a dropping of the pelvic floor, along with an extension of the spine and a lateral expansion of the ribs.

Can you imagine the amount of oxygen in your system if your breathing were that full all day? How about the benefits to the spinal column and the function of the brain through improved movement of the cranial bones and cerebrospinal fluid? Not to mention the increased relaxation in your mind and body. Remember as well, that the diaphragm actually functions to process emotion and experience.

Often, due to early teachings that emotions, fears and trauma must be repressed, the natural emotions arising are not processed in the diaphragm and the body takes steps to store them within its tissues. The result can be tension, pain and dysfunction, as these energies change the function of the areas where they are stored.

The incredible power of the breath struck home when working with my mare, Diva. Typically as slow as molasses, a stressor could literally send her into a panic, making her dangerous to herself and those around her. Of course, my first response had been to tense up and stop breathing, which Diva took as a sign that she was indeed about to be eaten by the piece of paper that had just blown by! Thankfully, I had just been introduced to the power of breathing and grounding. I began to breathe deeply and focus on my feet, with an emphasis on the out-breath and a focus on letting go of our collective anxiety. Over time, she began to calm noticeably around prior stressors, taking time to think before responding and sometimes even becoming curious. I'll often have my clients breathe deeply around their animals, which has the added bonus of calming and focusing everyone and allowing their experience together to be as relaxing as possible.

What a powerful exercise breathing is!

Here is a great exercise for a short and sweet breathing ritual to add some goodness to your day.

Exercise: Taking a deep and connected breath

Start by gently placing your hands over the base of your ribs on the diaphragm and connecting with your breath. I like doing this exercise while lying on my back, but sitting or standing work as well. For 10 deep, full breaths, notice everything about the quality of your breath. (And yes, it's very natural to lose track, especially when you're first starting. Keep coming back to your breath with lots of patience.)

Continue breathing in this way for 2-3 minutes (it may feel like an eternity when you're starting out!). This exercise takes patience and practice.

While you're breathing as deeply and fully as possible, ask yourself a few questions (it's a little like tapping your head and rubbing your belly)…

1. Is your in-breath the same length as the out-breath?

2. Is there a feeling of restriction in your body or mind at any point in the breath cycle?

3. Do you feel movement under your hands at the diaphragm?

4. Does taking a deep, full breath relax you or stress you out?

5. Do you prefer to breathe through your nose or mouth?

6. How does your animal(s) respond to your breathing?

Now move your hands to your chest at the collarbone. Take a few breaths while holding this area, again noticing anything about the breath.

Is your chest moving or still?

As the range of motion of your breath opens up, the chest will lift and open slightly with each inspiration.

Next, notice any shifts in your spine:

Is it expanding/moving or motionless?

The spine is actually designed to extend slightly on the in-breath and relax back into position on the out-breath. If you have a partner present, ask them to place their hands on your spine in two places about a foot apart. What do they notice?

Do their hands move apart from each other as you inhale and then back towards each other as you exhale?

Bring your awareness to any tension in your body.

What happens when you focus on releasing tension on the out-breath and creating space in the area on the in-breath?

What other changes do you notice when you place your full attention on your breath?

Notice what happens for your animal(s).

How does their breathing cycle and general state of being shift when your breathing cycle changes?

Spend 3-4 minutes daily practising deep and conscious breathing, as well as drawing your awareness back to your breath as much as possible during the day.

Take this practice with you in the car, to work, to the gym, out walking, while you eat, and definitely before bed. By practicing daily, you are setting down new and positive neural pathways in your brain and creating welcome patterns of relaxation and balance. You will also notice that your animals will begin to feel more peaceful and relaxed—an awesome bonus!

How does this relate to navigating our pet's final transition? The breath, with its superpowers in processing emotion, bringing us into the present and helping us chill, can change everything about how we are able to "be" at this challenging time. We become more able to be present for our animals, to tune into what they are needing, to be with our many emotions as they arise, and to honour our own unique and perfect way of moving through this difficult and growth-filled time.

Chapter 4

Furry gurus

Our lives are jam-packed with transitions: birth, death, new jobs, new relationships, beginnings and endings. In fact, it is rare that a day passes where we don't encounter some form of transition. They are both annoying and inevitable. A transition is defined as: the process or a period of changing from one state or condition to another.

It has been scientifically proven that the thing we humans will fight most to preserve is familiarity, otherwise known as sameness. For the majority of us, even the thought of change, whether perceived as positive or negative, makes our heart rate go up a few notches and the adrenaline rush through our veins.

So, when our precious family pet develops an illness or simply starts showing their years, we often experience stress—and a lot of it. If you're anything like me (and since you're reading this, I'm guessing you are), your pets are your family. We adore our animals, sometimes more than the people in our life, and even the thought of losing them can fill us with overwhelming emotion and a sense of dread.

I'm about to deliver a little tough love. The way we do one thing is the way we do everything. Here's how this old adage works when it comes to transitions. If we have a hard time with transitions in our life in general, chances are we are going to have a hard time handling transitions involving our animals, especially when it comes to death and dying. This is because we will tend to use the same strategies for one transition as we do for all of them. So, the first essential thing we need to look at and develop effective strategies for is how we handle transitions and change. Honing our skills in navigating transitions is a must, especially as animal lovers.

There are many factors that contribute to or detract from the development of this "skill," including what we're carrying from our ancestral lineage, our role-models as a child, and any cultural conditioning, along with our level of emotional intelligence and sensitivity. For example, many of us were taught as children to not think or talk about the subject of death and dying - that it is an inappropriate subject for discussion. The adults in our life modeled to us that denial and suppression are appropriate and helpful strategies when it comes to this taboo subject and so, it is little wonder that we decided to continue employing these strategies in our lives and with our loved ones.

As we grow up, we come to realize that death is inevitable, yet we may not have been given helpful modeling to know how to "be" throughout this transition and, in particular, afterwards. It is more than likely that the whole business terrifies us, let alone talking about it or asking for support. We then turn to various coping mechanisms as a way of holding things together, but we know deep down that there is something big missing from the equation. These patterns are just not giving us the resolution and feeling of peace we are deeply craving. And the truth is that they can't.

If we're really honest with ourselves, how many times in life do we just employ outdated coping mechanisms from our childhood and unconscious cultural conditioning to handle life? These strategies are familiar and may have worked for a time, but chances are they have held us back from the life we want and the type of connections we're wanting to create and experience. This is the very nature of a coping mechanism, which is designed with the sole purpose of helping us survive by getting our base needs met in whatever way necessary. They are, by their nature, not designed with a thriving and awesome life in mind. Rather the opposite actually, with their design based on the acceptance of an unfulfilling, limiting and "just getting by" kind of life. Sucky stuff indeed.

We may be familiar with some of our most well-used patterns or we may be completely unaware of them. Either way, they are playing out in all sorts of odd ways, generally being triggered by a specific type of experience. When it comes to these patterned behaviours, we operate in much the same way as a computer. When X experience happens, the result is Y pattern. This pattern will continue to play itself out like a broken record every time X happens, that is, until something shifts for us on the inside. To truly change how we handle transition, we've first got to change these out-of-date patterns that are just not cutting the mustard (I've always wanted to say that!).

One of the amazing things about our animals is that many of our transitions involve them—coming into our home, house training, illness and death—and each offers us an opportunity to do things differently. Every time something changes in our relationship with our animals, we have another opportunity to give something new a try.

The animal-steward relationship is actually the perfect testing ground for the new tools we're about to learn and the new ways of being we're getting ready to implement. Why? Well, have you ever known an animal to judge, smirk or criticize? And they most definitely don't hold a grudge or a grievance or try a guilt-trip on for size. They prefer to live smack dab in the middle of the present moment. They will not be upset if you set a boundary, sit for five minutes with them just breathing, or take a moment or five before trying out a way of communicating that potentially feels better for both of you. You'll probably find the opposite is true—it will seem like they've been waiting for you to figure this out all along and are overjoyed to be present for the change. You may even notice them showing shifting signals like licking, chewing and yawning to let you know that something new and great is happening and they are loving it!

Every time your consciousness shifts even the slightest bit, your animal will feel it. In fact, if you had your own personal cheerleading squad dancing and singing and backing you up, your animals would be at the front of the bunch shaking their tail feathers. This is because they are positively affected by every bit of healing you do. Just as the tiniest pebble can produce ripples in a pond, the tiniest bit of healing and transformation in you will produce positive changes in everyone and everything around you. Every one of us has seen the negative side of this effect firsthand in our animals when we are stressed out and determined not to show it, so just imagine what can happen when we begin to relax and get fully real on a deep and lasting level.

If you want to see this magic firsthand, spend some time with a horse or two. Horses are often used in therapeutic settings because of their incredible ability to reflect our emotions, both suppressed and expressed, back to us. As a prey animal, they are intrinsically wired to read the most subtle cues in those around them, picking up on nuances that are often undetected by humans. The moment something changes in you when you are around a horse, the shift is palpable, with the horse acting like a barometer and giving immediate and, often, obvious feedback. They are also skilled lie detectors, so they can be a great mirror for how "real" or authentic we are being in any moment. And because of their powerful connection to the heart, they are skilled at bringing you back to your own, a necessary and potently healing journey on your way to resolution and wholeness. There are many facilities worldwide offering opportunities to learn from horses in this way, an experience I highly recommend for the curious and dedicated animal lover.

Animals are great mentors and role models on rolling with transitions gracefully. Just watching them doing their thing can give you some awesome new strategies for moving through transitions. Have you ever watched a dog make a new friend, leave an old neighbourhood or move to a new country? They think it's the best thing ever! Even cats, who are a bit more fussy when it comes to transitioning, tend to settle and feel at home relatively quickly. When they do have an issue, it is usually something that can be cleared up in a healing session or two. Not so with most people. I have known people who have been away from their birthplace for over 40 years and still don't feel at home. There are countless human beings who die, quite literally, of a broken heart that never healed, and others who pass over to the other side still resenting a family member they haven't talked to in 20 years. Human beings are particularly skilled at holding on to the past, to old grievances, and to a deep and often painful longing for the way things used to be.

So, what do animals do in their day-to-day life that we don't? And moving into a bigger, more expansive question: how do animals experience their lives with us and at the end of their days?

Animal wisdom

This question has been one that has both fascinated and frustrated me endlessly throughout my 35 years. Because when we think of what our animals and their ancestors have moved through—their trauma and heartbreak paralleling our own throughout the ages—it can be hard to fathom the depth of connection and the powerful love that we share. And yet, it is beyond questioning that our lives are inextricably linked with those of our animals and that there is something truly divine and magical about the relationships we share with them.

This fascination with the way animals move through their lives and what they do differently has led me to a lifelong experiential study of how animals experience life and, particularly in the context of this book, how they experience death. My work over the last decade has allowed me the sacred experience of looking under the surface and into the depths of animals' consciousness and the nature of their connection with us, their humans. And what is below the surface is fascinating, indeed.

Cats, dogs and horses—and many more furry, scaly and feathery friends—join us willingly on this journey through life, keeping us laughing and lighthearted through even the hardest of times, and showering us unendingly with the type of unconditional love we yearn for from our fellow humans. Each one brings their own gifts, sharing with us their knowledge of tribe, transitions, grace and unconditional love. They are some of our most important, albeit humble, teachers on this journey called life, although we don't always see them that way.

Since we're on the topic of changing our perception, I invite you to begin to see your animals and your connection to them through this new lens, if you haven't done so before. Your previous experiences with them will more than likely start to make way more sense! It's amazing how all of my experiences with my animals, even as far back as childhood, gained new significance and clarity with this new understanding. With the help of our animal teachers, we can develop a deeper understanding of animal consciousness and, as an added side benefit, of human consciousness. What amazing beings we are lucky enough to spend our lives with!

My current understanding of animal consciousness encompasses what I consider the tip of the iceberg, and I feel blessed and honoured to continue to peer into this deep well of wisdom on a daily basis. It seems that along with the natural consciousness that each animal innately possesses (which differs for every species and varies significantly even within a species), there is something deeper still. Being so closely connected to human beings and our responses to the world, domesticated animals can experience many, if not all, of the states of human consciousness and the accompanying emotions. In a sense, they hold and reflect back to us our level and state of consciousness as human beings, guiding us slowly but surely towards a more evolved, loving and harmonious existence. At the same time, they are moving through their own story and learning their own unique life lessons. In essence, they choose us to be in their lives just as much as we choose them. And that is just plain cool.

Each species provides us with a different type of mirror to experience our consciousness as human beings.

Alright, this is where it starts to get really interesting. Over the years, I've seen different patterns arise in different species—the way they love us and teach us, as their humans, can look very unique depending on the species. So let's get started, shall we? Jumping to the head of the line, not surprisingly, are the wonderful beings that are our dogs.

Dogs, in their essence, would like to take on everything for us, so that we as their pack leader can be healthy and happy. They are loyal to a fault to their tribe (that would be us), putting our needs before their own without question. They desire more than anything to fulfill our needs and are dedicated to this task, whether it be a physical need, such as feeling less pain or stress, or a deeply ingrained emotional pattern requiring release or healing. They are unconditionally loving and uncompromisingly dedicated, often to their own detriment. Illness or imbalance in your dog(s) can be a good indication that you or someone else in your "pack" is not well, on a physical, emotional or energetic level, or that something in their world requires balancing.

Toxicity, allergies, digestive discomfort and arthritis can all be indicators of stuck or toxic energy manifesting in their physical body. Once the human pack member is able to recognize the pattern, pain, or stagnancy, the dog no longer needs to hold it and can return to a state of wellness. Often, a massage, energy work or flower essences can be powerful healing tools to aid them in letting go of any accumulated stagnation. With their deep and unconditional devotion to their people, dogs can be one of the hardest animals to heal, as they are often significantly energetically entangled with their human pack leaders. No guilt is required here - these canine angels happily lay themselves on the line for us and consider it an honour to do so. All they ask in return is your love and praise for a job well done.

When it comes to their final transition, dogs can have a very difficult time letting go. This is most often due to their intense devotion to their pack and their respective job(s). You see, almost all dogs have a job or two, or in the case of border collies, about 20! And they will decide on the majority of their job descriptions themselves, sometimes (if I can get a little woo-woo on you) being designated for their most important jobs long before they are born on Earth and become an integral part of your family. These particular jobs often include taking care of you and your family and making sure no one is hurt, which is why dogs are so sensitive to conflict and to ill-ness, and why they have such a difficult time passing over. I often work with dogs who stick around until they literally can no longer function because their devotion to their family is so deep. They are often terrified to cause pain or hurt in their people or to abandon their role, do-ing whatever they can to keep this from happening. When we can release them from their jobs and their commitment to us with love and gratitude, it allows them to make their final transition more easily and gracefully.

Dogs will very rarely make their final transition on their own, almost always requiring veterinary assistance to complete their passage. As their steward, it can be diffi-cult, if not intensely frustrating, to gauge the perfect tim-ing for this transition, as many dogs will hang on long after their physical state has deteriorated into discomfort and weakness. Working closely with a trusted veterinarian or animal communicator, or committing to your own intuitive training, will ease this frustration and confusion greatly. On a positive note (because you might just need one after all of that rather heavy stuff), dogs will continue their connection with you energetically long after their passing, taking up the role of a canine guardian angel, keeping other family dogs in line, and making sure their beloved human is taken care of and supported during their transition and far beyond it. Their intangible presence is often palpable, if you allow yourself to feel it.

Alright, let's move from dogs onto a very different kettle of fish: cats. **Cats**, as you might have guessed, reflect back to us in a very different manner. They are much more subtle and discreet about their teaching, resorting to more dramatic methods if change is slow to occur. They are not the easiest or kindest of teachers, that's for darn sure, and, if anything, they cultivate incredible patience in their humans! If you have a cat, you know exactly what I mean. Cats are brilliant energy workers, holding powerful space for the processing and movement of energy, emotions and patterns no longer serving us. Their purr, studied countless times over the years in reference to its healing potential, is thought to bring balance and harmony to the body and to the energy field surrounding it.

If you watch your cat closely, you can often gain very obvious hints as to which areas of your body require balancing. They will tend lie directly on the area that they feel is the highest priority. My cat Smoochie used to sleep in only two places, directly on my chest and right at the top of my head, balancing my heart and crown chakras—essential balancing for the work I was doing with my clients. He would also lie on all my human clients during their sessions, finding strategic spots that matched up with what was arising in the session to be balanced.

In my experience, cats don't tend to take on "baggage" in the way our dogs do. Cats are fundamentally selfish, putting themselves before others, not in a bad way, but in the spirit of incredible self-love. They are warriors and wanderers, concerned with freedom, wildness and fun.

That said, I have met a number of what I refer to as dog-cats in my travels (cats who carry a consciousness much more similar to dogs than cats), and vice versa, cat-dogs (dogs who are much more like cats than dogs). My whippet, B, was one such dog, moving through life in a way that bore an uncanny resemblance to cat consciousness. For most cats, keeping their bodies and energy systems well-aligned and balanced is imperative to shifting or releasing any energy that they no longer need or that isn't serving them. A cat with a spinal imbalance, stagnant or stuck energy, or a slow-flowing meridian can be quite grumpy—a fact you often find out after they have reacted to your touch or another stimulus at lightening-fast speed. Having a great support team, complete with someone who is capable of working on the energetic level, can go a long way to increasing the quality and longevity of their lives.

In their final transition, maintaining their solitary nature, cats will often find a space to curl up, either inside or outside, and let go. If this is not the case, the timing for their final transition (or the need for an immediate consultation with your veterinarian) is generally quite obvious, as they will stop eating and drinking and choose to sleep instead, or they will vocalize incessantly to inform you of their discomfort. Cats tend to adapt easily to this transition, having a deep understanding of and connection to the energetic realms. They can often be found in your peripheral vision even after their passing, an indication of their rather excellent sense of humour.

Horses, as far as consciousness is concerned, seem to be a rather fascinating combination of cat and dog consciousness, although never tell them that! Horses are the most regal of beings and like to be thought of as such. Like cats, horses hold onto baggage and "stuff" only when it is required for the owner to learn from. Like dogs, their relationship with their tribe is crucial; however horses, as prey animals, have a very strong drive for survival, which can mean that they will exclude an "unsafe" owner from their herd. This may include someone who is unable to be a strong, confident leader due to fear, an inability to create boundaries, or emotional reactivity. Although they put their tribe above themselves, they are very choosy about who is included in said tribe.

In my experience, horses are the most clear and powerful reflection of human consciousness through their strength of connection with the window to the soul, the heart. My horse, Diva, for example, can sense my energy before I walk out of my house in the morning to feed her. Her instincts are impressively sharp, and her ability to pick up on subtle energies is amazing and even a little annoying. With horses, especially horses like Diva, you can't get away with anything. Any resistance, pain or emotion not acknowledged in my body or mind will be almost immediately reflected by her back to me in a variety of interesting ways, which we'll touch on in a moment. But first, let's talk about incongruency, because it is one of the things that annoys horses the most, and is also one of their biggest lessons for us as humans.

Incongruency is the state in which our outside self does not match our inside self, or the thought does not match the action. Let me put this in context to help you understand why horses are so sensitive to incongruency in others.

Imagine a bear wandering through the woods. The bear is full of berries and meat, with no room left for hunting horses. The herd of horses he wanders past are more curious than scared, sensing his fullness. This bear is congruent, with his wandering matching his contented feeling inside. On the other hand, imagine the same bear walking by, this time ravenous with hunger. The way he walks by is identical, yet his thoughts tell another story—he is on the hunt. The horses are off and running, not interested in ending up as lunch.

The feedback from a horse to a person whose thoughts and emotions don't match their actions or behaviour is similar. Most horses will become understandably nervous at the disconnect between the truth and what we are actually expressing. It is no wonder that self-development facilities are being created across North America that honour horses for these natural instincts to show us exactly where we are and how "real" we are being.

When it comes to their health, horses benefit greatly from structural work, including massage, energy work and chiropractic, to balance and harmonize the physical and energetic elements in their bodies. They tend to hold tension and imbalance in their structural systems, in part because of their role as our riding companions. They can also be incredibly susceptible to stress and environmental challenges, often manifesting as digestive or immune issues.

In their final transition, it is rare for horses to let go by natural causes. Their prey animal instincts predispose them to hanging on well into old age, barring colic, disease or an accident, so as their steward, it will often be up to us to make the final call with the help of our veterinarian and support team. It is a priority to them that their herd is present if possible, including you, if not during, then most definitely after they have passed.

Once a herd mate has made their transition, the herd needs time to grieve and let go of their mate, in reflection of the grief of their person. They will often stand over the body or grave for hours and sometimes days, as part of the rite of passage and grieving process. Horses have a strong instinctual nature and carry the roots and rituals of their wild ancestors with them, despite their long domestication. As such, many continue their death and dying rituals as a legacy of their many generations running wild, grieving their dead with intense love, commitment and reverence. They will do the same if their herd mate is a human.

Pretty cool, huh? Our animals are truly incredible beings. And of course, birds, reptiles, rabbits, guinea pigs, hamsters and more have countless gifts and teachings, if we look closely enough.

I'm constantly struck by what a gift it is to share our lives with animals of all shapes and sizes. In fact, showing them gratitude, for being our friends, teachers and much more, is a powerful and essential step on our journey with them. It is also essential to acknowledge their natural animal consciousness, those things required by our animal to feel safe, comfortable and supported. A dog, for example, desires a pack leader who is able to set and maintain consistent boundaries for themselves and those around them. A horse requires an aware, grounded and trustworthy leader, capable of guiding them through this often crazy world unharmed.

There are always two parts of an animal that we need to account for—their natural consciousness as a living, breathing, Earth-bound animal and their higher consciousness as a soul or spirit. These parts are constantly interfacing and, in reality, are completely inseparable. As an owner, it is important to honour both parts as vital and indispensable, and find unique ways to fulfill the needs of our whole animal.

Shall we get into how we go about doing that, especially when it comes to death and dying?

Love every minute

Here's a part of it. One big reason our animals are here on Earth is to teach us how to enjoy every moment, even the uncomfortable ones. And death and dying are about as uncomfortable as it gets. I've confirmed with several other animal intuitives my hunch that one of our animals' biggest teachings for us as humans is how to gracefully navigate death and dying, since it is an area that can cause us some of the most intense pain and suffering possible. Observing our animals as they move through the experience of death and dying can help us begin to understand how to shift our own experience of this challenging time.

Almost every animal I have worked with before, during and after the time of their passing is accepting of this inevitable transition, many times even relaxed. In contrast, most of us fight our own death tooth and nail, struggling against the inevitable with every ounce of energy we still possess. The more you can step into seeing your animals as teachers, the more you will able to learn from and listen to them, and the easier these transitions will become.

After over a decade of connecting with animals and their humans and experiencing the countless nuances of this fascinating relationship, one thing has become abundantly clear: animals have life pretty much figured out. You only have to glance at your cat sunning himself next to his full food bowl to know it. And pretty much every animal I've met is amazingly accepting of their final transition. We humans, however, often have a tougher time rolling with the ever-changing rhythms of life. So what do animals do that we don't? And why are they so good at surfing the waves of this adventure called life and its inevitable end?

A dog's life

It's time to dive into why animals are potentially way more well-adjusted than most people. I don't mean this as an insult in any way; we only have to look at our dog's life to know the truth. My dog, for instance, has six different nap spots in my house, which she moves between depending on the location of the sun's rays, heating sources and me throughout the day, sleeping peacefully at each one. Meanwhile, I can be full of tension, biting my nails, forgetting to breathe, worrying about the future and holding onto various unchangeable situations from the past. The irony does not escape me. Animals have got this stuff figured out and not just because they aren't paying the bills! That's why, at this moment, we're going to address our inner control freak, because believe me, we've all got one, especially when we're adamant in saying that we don't. And yes, I can completely hear you through these pages, because I'm a control freak like that.

I'll admit it, I've got an inner control freak. In fact, there is a part of me (which is thankfully quite small these days) that feels the need to exert control over pretty much everything. This part of me has been conditioned since childhood to believe that if things are not under her control then they could go badly. And I really don't want things to go badly. When I follow this belief and the subsequent need to control something back to its source, there is always the same feeling lurking there. Yes, you know the one—fear. This is the part that wonders what awful things could and would happen if we actually let go of this suffocating vise-grip on our life and the lives of those around us. And this part of us is quite certain that if we let go of control, our world will completely fall apart and everything will be a huge mess. Ring a bell? Meet your inner control freak.

It has been said that all that's needed for the perfect thing to take place is the space for it to happen. So often with our animals, we smother them and any space needed for them to reach their potential or make their own choices. We may restrict our animal's activity because we perceive that something bad or uncomfortable might possibly happen to them, especially as our animal begins to show signs of aging and behaviour that is out of the norm. More than any other time in their life, we feel the intense desire to control the outcome and all possible negative factors during their final transition. This may look like constantly rushing our animal to the vet with the slightest issue, starting them on various medications, restricting their favourite activities for fear of a setback, or implementing 10 different healing modalities at once. Fear rears its head, and all the worst-case scenarios play before our eyes like a videotape. At this point, all we want is to fix everything and do whatever it takes to make everything the way it was, which, in the case of aging, is often impossible.

Don't get me wrong—all this care for our animals is awesome, but when it's motivated by fear and fueled by our own anxiety, it can put the entire household into a fear-based tailspin, not to mention the pressure we inadvertently put on our animal to "feel better."

This is the moment to change the pattern. Be completely honest and ask yourself: Is there any part of this situation that is out of my control regardless of my actions? How can I hold space for my animal without trying to control every tiny nuance of the situation, especially those things that are out of my control? To clarify, holding space means to create a metaphorical or energetic space where there is no judgment and no need to fix or change what is happening. It is a space where we can learn to trust in the process and how things want to unfold naturally, without our control. This is not an easy task, akin to loosening our death grip from the steering wheel of life and adopting a more trusting, relaxed outlook.

Remember, there is a difference between fear that is created out of a need to control and fear that is based in intuition or a sense of knowing. If the fear you are experiencing is founded in an intuitive or instinctual sense, it is important to honour it. But if it is your conditioning and deeply ingrained patterns taking the driver's seat, remind yourself to take a deep breath, and then another and another, breathing into the discomfort and facilitating the release of fear, tension and much more. Obviously, there is the possibility that the worst could happen. No matter how much you prepare, how much you control, this could be the case. But when you allow yourself to let go of your need to completely control the outcome, there is just as much opportunity for something unexpected and totally amazing to occur that you could have never predicted. In the releasing of control is where all the magic happens. And the same is true for our beliefs.

Before we dive deeper into a conversation about belief systems, let's first unpack exactly what a belief system is. Essentially, a belief is anything that describes a part of your concrete understanding of the world and how it works. Our beliefs and their development are influenced by countless factors, with the most influential being genetics and familial influence, cultural upbringing and life experience. These factors form and influence our perception of our world and our experiences in it. For example, a belief that "the world is a dangerous place" could have been formed through my mother's experience during my fetal life, shaping both my view of and truth about the world in potentially limiting ways, and my subsequent experience of it.

In essence, beliefs are powerful things, capable of changing our reality. In my experience, an animal will tend to live up to the belief(s) we have about him. So, if we believe him incapable of healing his own body, running safely with a herd or pack, or finding his own balance and confidence during the aging process, then this will probably be the case. If we can hold space for the possibility of unlimited and surprising potential, there is a great chance that we will be surprised by how capable our animal is, even during their final transition. This way of being can be way less stressful than trying to constantly control everything, particularly those things that are, by their nature, out of our control. At first, it's going to feel a bit like operating without a safety net, but try to trust me when I say that you are most definitely not. Like anything, we can start with small doses, releasing our grip on the easier stuff first and then working up to the more challenging as we gain momentum and confidence. The things that are completely and obviously out of our control to change or fix are a great place to start. For a little more help in this area, I would highly recommend the book *Daring Greatly* by the amazing Brene Brown. One of the coolest parts about all of this is that as we let go of our control and gain trust, our tension levels will start to lower, and our animals will be way more relaxed and content too!

So how do we know if our inner control freak is taking over? A great way to tell what part of us is making the decisions is to pay attention to our level of tension and our breath.

When we are feeling fearful, which is the underlying motivation in control, this emotion creates contraction in the body, otherwise known as tension. This is a coping mechanism created at the beginning of humans' stint on earth, designed as an excellent way to escape saber-tooth tigers and the like. Back then, when we felt fear, there was an associated survival-focused physiological response—blood would rush to our muscles, along with a powerful sympathetic nervous system surge, allowing us to run or fight for our life. Now, this tension-building physiological response arises for everything from driving the kids to school to preparing Christmas dinner to taking an exam. The result is the experience of eternal and ever-building tension in the body, a state that many consider to be normal, a rather sad reality nowadays.

For better or worse, this tension-filled, on-edge feeling has become familiar to many of us. But there's hope! When we can get in touch with the tension levels in our body and use our breath to encourage relaxation in these areas, not only do our muscles get a much-needed break but everyone else in our life does as well. The reality is that when we're in a relaxed state we're always more fun to hang out with than when we're in a fearful state. That's just a fact. Happily, the more relaxed we are, the more we are able to access the emotion that goes along with a sense of expansion, namely love. Love is an emotion, but it is also so much more than that, and the experience of it in our body feels like openness and freedom. In other words, it feels good.

When we allow tension to be released from the body, we allow ourselves to go from a state of constant high alert to lovingly laid-back. And when our decisions and choices come from this place, when they just feel good, it's a win-win for everyone.

Try this exercise to let go of tension:

Begin by taking several deep breaths into your belly. During this exercise, we'll be bringing your awareness to the tension levels in your body. Remember, it takes time to develop this awareness, so this is the perfect time to cultivate patience and acceptance for yourself and where you're at. Wherever you are in the process is perfect. If you feel any inner critics creeping in and giving you a hard time, you have my permission to tell them to take a hike.

Now, starting at the top of your head and face, draw the breath into this area, imagining that you are creating space for relaxation. On the out-breath, imagine any tension in those areas melting away. Continue for two to three deep breaths in each area, taking the time to zero in on any areas of holding or noticeable tension, and imagining these areas unwinding just like a ball of yarn, one knot at a time. Do the same thing now for the back of the head, and continue slowly and methodically into the neck, shoulders, arms, wrists and hands (each side), upper back and chest, lower back and abdomen, hips, upper legs, lower legs and feet (each side). Spend at least two full breaths in each area. Finish off with two to three full breaths reaching the entire body and melting away any remaining tension that is ready to be released.

Practice this exercise at least once daily to increase body awareness and encourage relaxation in the whole body. Remember, old habits are hard to break, so if your tension returns almost immediately, don't be discouraged. A daily practice allows new neural pathways to form and gradually shifts the body into a state of increased relaxation more and more of the time. Notice any changes in the behaviour or emotional states of those around you, especially your animals.

Notice what happens when you begin to relax and let go of control, little by little. And remember, it's not necessary to let go of all control; healthy and balanced control is essential. But the difference is this: healthy control comes from a space of love, like when I stand up as a trustworthy leader for Diva and ask her to do certain things to stay safe. I do this from a place of loving her deeply and wanting to create safety for her in a very human and challenging world, as opposed to controlling her behaviour and actions from a place of fear, guilt, anger or worst-case scenarios. The same would be true of an animal lover who controlled and managed the levels of stress present in their animal's environment—this is essential as the steward of their animals. An example of unhealthy control would be not allowing a healthy dog to interact with other healthy, balanced dogs for fear of conflict or injury, or because of a belief like "other dogs are dangerous" or a negative experience in the past. This limits the experience of both the dog and the human. I have experienced many, sometimes challenging, lessons in this area of discernment between healthy and unhealthy control and have my fingers crossed that I've finally sorted out the difference!

Healthy expression

Before we continue, it is important to recognize that our need to control everything in our world often arises from a need to control ourselves and our experience. Generations of conditioning can create strong programming insisting that full expression of our feelings is not appropriate, acceptable or OK. This need to control yourself and your way of being in the world can ripple out into your life in many ways—some helpful, some not very helpful at all. In terms of death and dying, full expression can be a terrifying thought, particularly if we are unsure exactly what that would look or feel like. A logical and highly controlled experience often appears to the better option, even if it means dangerous stifling of our expression, affecting our own health and the naturally emotional process of navigating transition. In other words, a part of our learning here in life is figuring out how to be healthily expressed and safe at the same time. It's completely possible, I promise!

Allowing our animals an outlet of free expression is a wonderful and gentle way to begin training our mind toward the idea that healthy expression is good—and it is safe. Letting them run, play and just be themselves, within reasonable boundaries and without stopping up their expression or needing to fix their behaviour, is a simple exercise with a huge pay-off. It literally begins to re-organize your mind, opening it up to the possibility that freedom of expression might actually be an awesome thing. Eventually, when you need to express something, your mind will understand how this can be safe and that you can allow the expression without trying to fix, change or stop it. But before we get into how we go about doing that, let's talk a little about guilt and shame, an essential conversation when we're exploring freedom of expression.

Guilt and its close cousin, shame, are from the same family as fear. For the moment, let's think of fear as the head honcho of this not-so-pleasant family. The reality is that we'll all experience these emotions on a fairly regular basis, and they are only going to intensify when we're faced with an animal who is nearing the end of their life. This is why we are going to unpack some of the big reasons these emotions exist in the first place, and how to work with them. I'm going to get a wee bit "out there" with you for a moment, so bear with me.

Whenever we experience guilt or shame, it is always overlaying fear. Always. Here's why. Guilt is bred from the feeling of not-enoughness or of being wrong in some way. Its root is the fear of rejection and abandonment and, if we follow that to its conclusion, death. You see, the fear of death is pretty much at the basis of everything we do. Every time we stop our expression or do something we don't want to do because we feel guilty or ashamed, it comes from a cascading path of fears that inevitably ends at our fear of dying. Crazy, huh? Is it any wonder that death is so hard to navigate? It is, quite literally, one of our greatest fears. No wonder we have an almost impossible time looking at it, much less talking about it or working with it.

In light of this, I invite you to try something: spend a day paying attention to what actually motivates you and your behaviour. Just one day. Be as curious and as honest with yourself as you possibly can, noticing when guilt or shame, or the avoidance of them, are directing your decisions and actions. The results might shock you. I would hazard a guess that the majority of our behaviour as human beings is, and has been, motivated by an attempt to avoid feeling guilty or shameful. The irony is that we usually do anyways. And the crazy part is how effective this form of motivation actually is. Ever experienced a guilt trip? Those things have been used with success for hundreds, if not thousands, of years for a reason. This leads me to my next invitation, and this one will probably be harder because it requires you to get completely real with yourself. Assess how often you use guilt and shame to motivate the behaviour of others. Yes, it's a little humbling, but this new awareness will be incredibly freeing for you and for those in your world.

So the big question is, how do you disentangle yourself from this rather vast web of guilt, shame and fear? Well, first off, watch your animals—they are almost immune to guilt trips and most, aside from some dogs, seem to move through life free of guilt and shame. How marvelous would that be? My cat Parker has been an awesome teacher on this level. He lives a completely guilt-free existence and is impossible to rein in. I've attempted guilt-trips and cat-shaming to no avail—he simply does what he wants. So, I've had to choose love and acceptance, with healthy boundaries (no you may not ninja leap at my face claws first when you're angry) and healthy control (because it's not safe for him in my human world if I'm not the leader), and that seems to work wonders!

When it comes to our animal's final transition, guilt and shame tend to rear their heads with even more intensity. We question our decisions: Should I have taken my animal to the vet sooner? Maybe there was something else I could have done? Am I making the right decision? We berate ourselves for our choices, particularly when it comes to timing and especially if our animal passed on tragically. We replay the same situation over and over in our head, feeling more and more guilty about what we should have or could have done. Can you relate?

Let me stop you right there. Because this is a downward spiral that doesn't go anywhere good. Guilt and shame, although they might feel helpful, are quite the opposite. They are destructive emotions, breaking down our hard-earned self-worth, our precious hearts and our beautiful, playful spirits. Yes, feel them, but from there, acknowledge them and the fact that they are not serving you, and let them go with love. Alright, rant over. Let's get back to some less heavy topics, like this awesome exercise for waking up your playful side with your animal.

Try out this exercise with your animals—the "hang out and just be" exercise...

Go to a dog park (or your enclosed back yard), or a safe and obstacle-free horse ring, if you are an equestrian. (For cats, this exercise can be done in the comfort of your own home, although most cats already operate from complete freedom of expression and you've more than likely come to accept that fact.) Bring some sort of musical device (e.g., iPod, walkman, radio or, better yet, a speaker system). Be sure that the area is all yours, with no other animals.

Allow your animal to go free if possible, taking them off their leash or removing their lead rope. Move around the area with your animal or just let them move about freely, breathing deeply and intentionally to release the need to control yourself or them. They might run, lie down, play, or just stare at you, waiting for further instructions.

If you feel the need to control creep in, notice and acknowledge it without judgment, take a deep breath and move back into the present moment. Have no plans and no agenda. Turn the music up and let yourself move freely around the space. Just see what naturally transpires and how your body wants to move. Notice how your animal responds to your movement—you may find they are initially a little nervous having such a different experience of you, but that they start to relax and unwind noticeably as you begin to do the same.

Here are a few other things to notice during this time with your animal:

• What emotions come up for you?
• Can you be with the emotions that are arising without judging or fixing them?
• Can you be with any emotions that are arising for your animal without judging or fixing them?
• Can you stay present and grounded while moving more freely through space?
• Can you allow your animal to let loose?
• Can you allow yourself to move freely?

Start with just a few minutes and work up to 30 minutes or however long you would like, because after the first few awkward times it's going to get a whole lot more fun. Remember, there are no rules. Yep, that's right, absolutely none.

When I first started doing this exercise with my mare, Diva, many years ago, it was terrifying for me. After all, I had been trained very traditionally in riding and it was rare to ever allow horses to go loose in a large area, even in a secure ring area. When we first started, I had worst-case scenarios running through my head like a movie reel. I was also completely unable to move my body freely because I was so scared of the judgment of others and of spooking Diva. Then we started to find our groove, moving through space together in completely new and different ways and having fun being plain silly. What I realized is that neither of us really knew how to play, or we had forgotten. In fact, big part of our journey together has been remembering how to play and have fun. Now we run through the fields together and I ride bareback, sometimes with no bridle at all. It is the most freeing feeling imaginable to stop caring what anyone else thinks, release any feelings of guilt and shame, and just dance to the beat of your own drummer with your beloved animal by your side. Speaking of which, let's continue learning about how our animals experience life and death, and what we can learn from them.

Sniffing out BS

And when I say BS, I mean both bullshit and belief systems. You see, animals are very sensitive and aware of thoughts, emotions and even beliefs in their environment. They have an uncanny ability to uncover incongruencies—the discord between the outward actions and the thoughts/emotions of those around them. In a sense, you could say they are brilliant readers of the mind, as well as every tiny nuance of body language that translates from our current emotional and mental state. Yes, it is a little unnerving when you first realize the truth of this—have our animals been reading our minds all this t i m e ? !

As their guides in this slightly crazy world, it is important to find a healthy balance between denial and healthy control. In other words, it is very important to be educated about how to cultivate, recognize and maintain health for our animals. After all, we are their stewards. This may look like keeping up on research about nutrition, learning a healing modality, working on ourselves, or taking a course in animal communication. Denying that our animals could be in any way affected by stress, their environment, aging or an accident can be potentially damaging. Herein lies a rather tricky balance!

As we've discovered, focusing intently on the countless awful situations that could befall our animal partner, and employing prevention strategies to "bubble wrap" them, can lead to similar trouble. Striking a healthy balance in this grey area between denial and control requires the rather humbling recognition that this is an area where we can all use some support, especially when it comes to navigating the aging process and our animal's final transition. This is a transition we should never expect ourselves to handle alone, although we often do exactly that. Just as our dog does with their pack and our horse does with their herd, gathering a trustworthy support network around us is essential to navigating any transition gracefully.

On that very important note, if we find ourselves being drawn repeatedly into old patterns and destructive ways of thinking, like a cart in a rut, this is a great time to ask for help. For example, if we experienced a particularly traumatic death of an animal companion in the past, we may find ourselves haunted by that experience and literally unable to move on. In this case, the thoughts, memories and emotions that are evoked can hold us prisoner until we find a way to be released from them. The shift possible in this type of circumstance with even a small amount of outside help is often huge, as it will affect us on all levels, often with great benefit and significant relief. Speaking from personal experience, I've learned that making ourselves a priority and receiving support in the form of body work, energy work and counseling creates a lightness that you have to feel to believe. And, most surprisingly, with the right support, we can literally change our entire perception or way of viewing the world, in a matter of minutes. And, as we're starting to find out, our perception of our experience is a huge piece of the puzzle.

Here's the annoying thing about perception, though. Sometimes, as much as we attempt to think positively, we find ourselves sidetracked by a mysterious force. Affirmations and positive thinking can be incredibly helpful, but we may have contradictory belief systems lodged in our subconscious mind that are derailing our attempts to experience the world in a different light. As I mentioned earlier, the subconscious mind is similar to the base of the iceberg, the part of us that we can't see but is there affecting things nonetheless. And as we move through life, we're like little sponges for all sorts of crap that we don't even know about. The crazy-making part of this lies in how profoundly all this unseen crap affects us. Let's just say that if our life keeps derailing at the same place or the same sucky thing keeps happening over and over, our unconscious beliefs might just be the culprits.

It's time to get really clear and honest about your current beliefs and conditioning. We all carry many beliefs and thought patterns about death and dying, some of them even completely opposing. Every single one of us sees this transition through a different lens, which makes for countless ways of moving through it. These beliefs have been created over a lifetime of experiences, cultural conditioning and role-modeling. The effect of our beliefs on our perception can be understood through the analogy of looking through a lens— one that is perfectly clear can become very foggy or difficult to see through. The filters created by our beliefs change our perception of our experience, creating reduced clarity, understanding and, often, a much more challenging time dealing with everything that our life is throwing at us.

These layers of out-dated beliefs and perceptions are often the most difficult to touch, not just because they are hidden, but because somewhere deep down we'd like them to stay that way. After all, these beliefs, limiting or not, make up the very foundation of our existence. And where there is a shaky foundation, there is most likely someone or something attempting to defend it from harm. The same goes for our out-dated beliefs making up a shaky foundation that we will do our darnedest to protect. In fact, we can gauge how fundamental a belief is to us by the amount of resistance we have to uncovering and exploring it. Add to all of this the fact that some of our outdated beliefs are just not very pretty to look at and it feels a whole lot easier to keep them under lock and key. It's little wonder the subconscious mind keeps them well hidden. It takes courage, humility and a good sense of humour to see and then release the beliefs that are limiting our experience of all parts of our life.

Happily, I've got some awesome news for you on this front. Remember our little chat about receiving support a few paragraphs ago? There have been many modalities developed, including the BodyTalk System, Emotional Freedom Technique and Psych-K, to help shift the limiting effects of our beliefs. There are many books on the subject, countless coaching programs, and a multitude of audio choices. What it all comes down to is this: our beliefs affect everything—our biology, our career, our ability to make and keep money, our relationships, and our experience of death and dying.

So what do you believe about death and dying? This area can be a veritable minefield of belief systems, some even contradictory. For example, we could have a conscious belief that says, "Death is a peaceful experience," but subconsciously hold a belief developed from a childhood experience insisting that "Death is full of suffering." When the experience of death and dying comes up, these two beliefs battle for position, with the subconscious belief almost always coming out victorious. It is one of the most unfair games of tug-a-war ever, with the subconscious mind towering over the conscious and willing to play dirty. This is why affirmations without the deeper work to back them up never quite cut the mustard.

What happens next is the scary part. The belief that wins will often draw to us a situation that resonates with and affirms that belief. So if the belief at the forefront is "Death is full of suffering," then we may find ourselves in a situation that happens to affirm that belief for us. Sucky right?

Take a moment and write down four or five limiting beliefs or "stories" that you have experienced around death
and dying. These may be things you have heard people
in your life say or that you have experienced. They may
also be related to your cultural upbringing (e.g., it is not
polite to talk about death).

1. _____

2. _____

3. _____

4. _____

5. _____

Notice how these beliefs, however wild and wacky, may
have created some of the experiences of death and dying
you have had up until now. What would your life look
like if these types of experiences no longer needed to be
part of it? Are you willing to let go of these belief systems that you now understand are limiting rather than
helpful? Often, all that is needed to shift these limiting
patterns is a willingness to bring them to the surface, to
see them and release them. Once we can understand
their effect on our experience, we are able to let them go.
Sometimes, more work is needed to completely heal

these patterns and it's time to book an appointment with a trusted professional. Whatever the case, it is important to be aware of the effects of our belief systems on our life, and to be open and willing to change.

When it comes to the transition of death and dying in our companion animals, our work in this one area can mean the difference between a highly traumatic experience and a conscious and peaceful one. Incredibly, as we do this work, any past experiences will also be transformed as we begin to see them through a different lens. This will allow the animal lover who is having difficulty letting go of a deceased animal or finding resolution, or is unable to bear the thought of another animal passing on, to have a different, clearer perspective on this transition and how their animal experienced it. This one shift in perspective can open the door for another animal or joyful opportunity to enter our life without resistance.

Unravelling time

As a species, human beings are acutely aware of time. Not only that, but we are aware of how much time we have left, and how much we would like to and should accomplish in this time. Words like *motivation, goals, deadlines* or even *rushed* would not exist without the perceived pressures of time. Another word that would be somewhat meaningless without the concept of time is *agenda*. One of the definitions of agenda is: a series of steps to be carried out or goals to be accomplished. Generally used to describe the organization of council meetings, the term agenda can also be a powerful way to describe our attitude towards our animals and their final transition. Hear me out on this.

Take a minute and think of the animals in your life. Then ask this question: "Do they experience time the way I experience time?" We know that they are intensely aware of their environment and what is happening in it, paying attention to the little details and somehow knowing exactly when their mealtime is. It is obvious, though, that animals do not check their watch routinely or consult their agenda planners and calendars to find out if they are on schedule or if they have somewhere important to be. They are up to more important matters, like paying attention to the present moment, eating, napping, hunting bugs, playing, grooming, licking their crotch, getting scratches and immensely enjoying their life. How cool would that be to just enjoy life?

What I've realized over a lifetime of fascination and observation is that animals are very aware that it is impossible to control most things that happen within their life. Instead they tend to go with the flow of what is showing up in each moment. This is the case when it comes to their final transition, a situation that, in many ways, is entirely impossible to control or predict. This is just one of the things that makes this experience so incredibly challenging to navigate—there is no plan. The unfortunate thing about agendas and plans is that inevitably there will be stress and suffering if things do not go as we had originally planned. And in all my time with animals, if I have learned one single thing, it is that things rarely, if ever, go as planned.

Don't get me wrong. I think planning can be very helpful in moderation. After all, life would be more than a little chaotic without a bit of structure to give it some backbone. We need that. And as the stewards of our animals, we know they definitely enjoy getting their meals, playtime and snuggles right on time. So there's no need to throw out our watches and clocks just yet.

The real trouble begins when we become reactive to something not going as planned or not fitting the strict agenda we have set out in our minds. This tends to be where the resistance and stress begins for ourselves, and subsequently, for our animals. When we are unable to adapt to changes to "the plan," we can easily miss and pass over important messages from our animals or spend too much time worrying, rather than connecting. For example, if our animal is aging, we may have an agenda requiring that they live forever, or at least for a very, very long time. This agenda might be based on believing that their presence makes us happy and that we won't be able to live without them. Our agenda can then take over our experience with our animal, especially as they begin the inevitable process of aging. We might try every therapy, veterinary procedure, pain remedy and anti-aging supplement we can find, to no avail. We may spend our time worrying, researching, and feeling anxious and frantic, rather than spending this time connecting with our animals and what they are needing. Our animal may be obviously very uncomfortable and displaying this physical discomfort through progressively extreme behaviours. Instead of paying attention to these messages, we might push through towards our goal of keeping him alive, effectively creating more stress on everyone concerned.

When we can step back and open our minds and hearts to the truth that our animal is preparing to make their final transition, we can begin to receive the information we need to make the best decisions for them. This may look and feel very different from what we had originally planned. To learn to let go of our personal agenda and listen with our hearts to our animals, allowing what needs to unfold to do so, are some of the most important skills to grow and develop in our role as steward of our animals. And annoyingly, they are also some of the hardest.

Let's include in this discussion about agendas the unique aging process of an animal. Our desire to set up an agenda around this unpredictable process is understandable. But no matter where this agenda originates—as it may have been created by someone else, like a veterinarian or another professional—our animal's health and happiness relies on our ability to see what is actually needed. Remember, what is *actually* needed might be very different from what we think they need.

I won't sugarcoat this—tapping into these needs requires very deep listening on many levels and a full release of any personal agenda, not always an easy task. Start by paying close attention to their body language. Maybe your dog begins placing a certain body part in front of you, a sign that a scratch or a massage would feel just lovely. Watching their eyes and subsequent body language will allow clarity on what type of touch they are requesting or how that touch feels. Maybe they have a certain spot that is absolutely off-limits, accompanied by behaviour that is out of the norm, like growling or nipping. This feedback is worth listening to; it is your animal's way of sharing their experience without words. It is important to explore this feedback and find the help needed to understand it, as these small imbalances can often be clues to a greater puzzle. In fact, animals are

constantly communicating with us through our subtle
senses, which we'll be learning to connect with and cultivate throughout these pages.

The subtle senses

So how do we start to pick up on what our beloved furry
bestie is putting down, especially if their body language
is not clear? By listening to our intuition. You might just
be shaking your head here and wondering what on earth
this has to do with agendas or any of what we've been
talking about. Let me be blunt: our intuition is the best
tool we've got when it comes to being in the moment,
navigating the challenging transition of death and dying,
and being the best steward to our animals. And contrary
to popular belief, we're all intuitive—it's not just for the
"gifted." I used to tell myself that story because I was
about as disconnected from my subtle senses of sight,
hearing, smell, touch and taste as I could be. I was quite
sure only certain people had the gift of being intuitive.
Not true. Here we are 12 years later and I've "communicated" with thousands of animals using that same intuition I was quite certain I did not have.

Yes, intuition is something that requires daily practice
and dedication, carving out quiet time and getting fully
present. And if you have any doubt that animals can and
do communicate on this level all of the time, I encourage
you to watch the incredible documentary *The Animal*

Communicator (I've included the link to my favourite part in the resources section).

Being in touch with our intuition is one of those things that makes all of us better stewards for our furry loved ones. It is a commitment to learning to communicate in their language, a communication system that goes far beyond body language. Start with the little stuff. If you get a sense that your pet is really not digging your current veterinarian or wellness practitioner, maybe it's time to seek out another one for a second opinion. Or perhaps you get a sense that you'd like a little more information or guidance on their current food. Maybe it's as subtle as moving their bed to a place that feels better for both of you. Pay attention to these subtle but significant messages. These are just some of the ways our animals communicate with us.

The more present we become with our animals, the more messages we'll start receiving. Just like tuning into the right radio station, we'll be amazed by the increasing clarity and connection it brings. Enjoying the unique journey that each day with our animal brings, rather than getting caught up in the end result, can positively transform your relationship, even in its last days. And if you want to dive deeper to further strengthen your intuitive skills, there are some incredible online and in-person animal communication courses out there to get you started. I have included a few of my favourites in the resources section at the back of the book.

An exercise in being free as a bird...

In this exercise you'll practice spending time with your animals without an agenda. What do you have to lose? Other than a whole lot of tension and maybe some wrinkles? Grab a lawn chair and sit in your horse's paddock or lie on the grass with your dog or cat. Relax, breathe deeply and perhaps even take off your watch.

Notice whether it is difficult or easy to be in the present moment, with no thoughts of the past or the future, or feeling that there is something to get done or achieve.

Can you get in touch with all of the sounds, textures, smells and sights around you?

Can you open up to your senses a little more with each breath, engaging in your experience more and more deeply, just as your animals do?

Be willing to consider that by getting to know your mind in this way, you are not wasting time. In fact, you are doing quite the opposite. You are connecting with the ways of your animal and creating strong foundations for trust, connection, and understanding, both now and in the future when they have made their transition.

See if you can allow your time together to be free of agendas, as well as fun, playful and relaxing.

Be a complete goof. Roll in the grass, gallop madly about, climb a tree, lie in the sun with arms and legs splayed. Just go with the flow of the moment, allowing life to move you, rather than the other way around.

Yes, I know, it's easier said than done. But like I said earlier, what do you have to lose?

Notice the change in both of your bodies when an agenda becomes the focus. If your animal displays stress in your time together, do your best to become aware of the source and curious, rather than pushing through.

Is this stress created by discomfort in his physical body, past trauma, or something he is mirroring for you? Be curious about and open to the possibilities, allowing yourself to receive feedback from your animal without judging it as negative.

It is remarkably easy to misinterpret an animal's poor or abnormal behaviour. If we are observing behaviour that is out of the ordinary for our animal, there is a good chance it is being caused by pain, disease or past trauma. This kind of feedback from our animal calls us to practice compassion and curiosity in order to arrive at an informed, intuitive and loving choice around how to proceed.

When my whippet, B, was in her final two years, I had some big inner work to do around one particular behaviour that drove me crazy—peeing in the house. What I came to realize is that I needed to strengthen my compassion muscles in a big way. I also need to become even more tapped into my subtle senses in order to understand what was really happening for her. During her final years, B was struggling, not only with cognitive dysfunction and encroaching blindness, but a decline in her sense of smell, making the lines between inside and outside the house understandably blurry. After a session or two on myself, I understood that what this situation required was love, understanding, intuitive connection and an effective plan to help my beautiful little gal out. Once these were in place, everyone (even my other animals) was happier.

When we can be flexible, connected and open-minded, understanding that nothing is really fully in our control, and that our carefully laid plans will more than likely change, we can navigate the challenging waters of the aging process with much more grace and ease. As we learn to adapt fluidly to these changes while keeping the happiness and health of both ourselves and our animals in mind, we will begin to enjoy the journey, whatever it has in store. The more connected we are to our subtle senses, a skill we'll explore more in the coming chapters, the more we can trust in our animals and in ourselves.

Cultivating trust

Animals seem to have an admirable grasp of the concept of "divine" timing. In essence, divine timing underlies an understanding that everything in our lives is happening exactly as it needs to, in perfect timing. It's very possible that an animal's lack of agenda or expectations has a whole lot to do with this balanced way of viewing the world, or maybe their innate ability to go with the flow. In contrast, with our human tendency to focus on control and comfort, it can be a challenging task for most of us to allow and accept the role of divine or universal timing in our lives—or, more precisely, to trust in the flow.

Several years ago, I had a call from a family whose cat was experiencing renal failure due to a blocked urinary tract and had been given only a few days to live. According to the vet, the cause of the failure was a mystery. My visit with this cat revealed a host of factors, almost entirely emotional and energetic, relating to the imbalances within his kidneys and bladder. When the owner asked if it would have been best to have me out earlier, when the problem was starting (even though they hadn't heard of me then), it was a great reminder for me of the concept of divine timing. For whatever reason, this part of this cat's healing journey needed to begin at this precise time. His health improved between visits, but he let me know after our second session that I was not to see him again for three weeks. Again, I questioned the timing, particularly for a cat who had only been given until the next day to live. Wanting a second opinion on his well-being, I recommended a very well-liked holistic veterinarian. The timing once again worked beautifully as a sought-after appointment opened up the next day. This lovely cat recovered well and his owners have a new understanding of timing, amongst other things!

So often, feelings of fear, worry, guilt, shame, regret, frustration and impatience come up around events and experiences whose timing was perfect and also entirely out of our control. It is not an easy thing to trust that the timing is being divinely orchestrated, especially when outward appearances suggest otherwise. The reality is that there are many things we just can't control, and we can either torture ourselves or accept and trust the timing. Personally, I much prefer option two, the one without the emotional and mental torture.

If you think back over your experiences, particularly those involving animals, are you able to see an inexplicable underlying force at work, with or without you controlling how things play out? Here's where we get a little more spiritual, because this underlying force can't be explained by logic alone. Brené Brown, in her book *Rising Strong*, explains it beautifully. "Spirituality," she shares, "is recognizing and celebrating that we are all inextricably connected to one another by a power greater than all of us, and that our connection to that power and to one another is grounded in love and belonging. Practicing spirituality brings a sense of perspective, meaning and purpose to our lives." She goes on to explain that spirituality and where we find it is a completely unique experience for each individual. I wonder if many of us, as animal lovers, find our sense of spirituality, or least a part of it, in our connection with our animals. So, divine timing, in essence, is based in a trust in our connection to something much bigger, a greater plan.

To ground this whole conversation back in the practical, it makes sense to go with the flow and trust in divine timing because it doesn't make energetic sense to be any other way. The phrase "resistance is futile" comes to mind. But the reality is that we will resist and fight the inevitable, particularly when it comes to death and dying. It is, for most of us, a natural and deeply challenging part of our process. This transition can feel almost impossible to swallow if the timing doesn't fit our plan and especially if our animal's death is sudden or traumatic. In this case, our animals seem to have a sense of timing that operates outside of any logical plan we may have for them. It may take months, years or more to digest an experience of this nature, and that is OK.

Over the last decade, I have received countless calls and emails about animal clients that have passed over. At first, I took these deaths quite personally, feeling as though I should have been able to make these animals better or fix them, as if I had failed them somehow. It was common for their people to feel the same way, as if there was something more they could do or something else they hadn't yet tried. Then I began to understand something very important—there was nothing to fix. How can it be anyone's job, especially mine, to decide for any animal what their path should look like? What if their healing process actually meant finally being able to complete their final transition with grace and ease?

Recognizing that our animals have their own divine timing does several things. First, it creates greater freedom of choice, for both ourselves and our animals. Second, it releases some of the fear that comes with making difficult choices for our animals around timing. And third, it bolsters understanding, acceptance and self-forgiveness.

Several years ago, my cat, Smoochie, developed a growth on his face just under the eye and beside the nose. It looked similar to a small crater and was in an area that was impossible to do surgery on without involving his eye or his sinuses. He was 16 years old and had been in my life since age 7, when he started licking my arm at the local SPCA and I fell immediately in love. I treated him and his growth in every way I knew how, trying everything other than surgery or chemotherapy. I trusted my intuition, consulted my team, did energy work, and searched for guidance. But still, his growth continued to grow. I felt varying emotions during this time, ranging from guilt to shame to flat-out confusion. After all, this was my career and my gift—I should be able to fix him!

Eventually the growth became so large and deep that it became infected, oozing pus and blood. It was obviously very painful and I kept it in check as long as I possibly could. Eventually, Smoochie stopped eating and slept most of that day and the next. It was obvious that he was on his way and he shared with me intuitively that he was ready. There was a part of me that found it incredibly hard to accept that my beautiful cat was saying goodbye. But, checking in with him through those last days, I could feel he was waiting for me to be ready to let him go. After much questioning of the timing, and consulting with Smoochie's wellness team, I had to let go of my expectations of myself and my agenda to "fix" him and accept that he was running his own show. And I had to accept that this was something I could not control, as much as I wanted to. That moment of acceptance and granting him permission to go was both challenging and liberating for both of us. I realized that my greatest gift to him was to honour his divine timing and his innate knowing of what he needed.

In doing this, I created a connection with Smoochie that stays with me to this day. It doesn't mean I don't miss and grieve the loss of him and his sweet, loving physical presence. I do, and it comes in waves. But I also feel deeply connected to him in the spiritual sense. Interestingly, my two-year-old cat, Parker, looks remarkably like Smoochie and has very similar mannerisms, something that fascinates me unendingly and, of course, opens up a whole other Pandora's box of questions.

When it comes to our animals, love is the most important thing: love of self, others and of the world. If you can get to a place of openness, love and trust in your heart and in your mind, many things will fall into place naturally, without struggle or effort. The timing already exists if we can trust and allow what needs to happen. The great thing about it is that wherever we are on this path is still perfect, whether we are trusting in the timing or not, so no regrets or guilt are required. When it all shakes out, the timing is always perfect. That's the wonderful thing about divine timing. The entire process of death and dying seems to be one of bringing us closer to the ones we love, and to a deeper understanding of what we hold dear and what is truly important and valuable to us.

Just as elephants stand over the body of their herd mate for as long as necessary, so too is there a timing for each of us and the loved one we are grieving. To drop into the realm of grief requires impressive courage—there is no road map for this journey, which is as unique as each person who is moving through it. It can be a period of intense discomfort as we allow ourselves to feel our emotions as they come up. It may look like many things,

from a single tear to a gush of mixed-up emotions to anger to disbelief. Whatever grief and loss looks like for
you, it is coming up to be felt, acknowledged, processed
and, eventually, released. Breathe, breathe and breathe a
little more. And most definitely, read the next chapter.

Chapter 5

Well, hello there, grief

"There are those, however, that are not frightened of grief: dropping deep into the sorrow, they find therein a necessary elixir to the numbness. When they encounter one another, when they press their foreheads against the bark of a centuries-old tree...their eyes well with tears that fall easily to the ground. The soil needs this water. Grief is but a gate, and our tears a kind of key opening a place of wonder that's been locked away. Suddenly we notice a sustaining resonance between the drumming heart within our chest and the pulse rising from the ground." —David Abram

Time to go there. We're ready. Take a deep breath, and then another. Let the Pandora's box that is your grief crack open ever so slightly. Better now than in the middle of the supermarket aisle or in a traffic jam. Better now than never. There's never a perfect time to work with the loss weighing heavy on your heart, your mind and your body. And you may never feel totally ready to navigate its depths. So let's begin. As my dear friend and grief expert, **Celeste Morris**, shares, grief is an integral part of life. In her powerful teachings, she honours grief and its potency in our lives.

In her beautiful words…

"Grieving is a part of our wildness. It is a part of life. It is an inherent part of our human nature. When we deny grief a place in our lives, we cut off our airflow, and we suffocate and disconnect ourselves from the very life that feeds us. Grief and Life are the same thing. They belong in the same house. To evict one is to separate yourself from your very nature."

She goes on to share something that I have long witnessed in myself and others:

"We have a cultural phobia around the whole subject of grief, death and loss. In our culture, grief, death and loss are not really talked about. No one prepares us to know what to do, what to say, how to support ourselves or others during a time of loss. Everyone experiences heavy emotions and difficult life experiences but rarely do we share what we are facing, in an honest way, with other people. More often than not, we're just doing our best not to show anyone how messed up we feel inside. We are immersed in a fast-paced culture that doesn't take the time or presence to exchange honest and candid conversation, let alone deep and meaningful connection.

We are trained to ride the surface and share only that which is pleasant."

I, like many of us, have found it easier to stay on the stoic side of grief, to leave my Pandora's box tightly clasped, to put my head down and power my way through it. Celeste and others have been instrumental in showing me another way, and I am still working at feeling fully comfortable with the countless and varied expressions that grief has in the world and our unique experience of it. It can be a profoundly messy and uncomfortable experience, a deep and thorough excavation of our very soul. And as I've personally discovered, it can also look subtle and soft, with just a tear or two shed. Every experience is what it needs to be. This is just one reason why I am so honoured to share the experience of Celeste and her husband, Bradley, in the passing of their beloved border collie, Sasha.

Sadly, men can feel even more restricted in their expression of grief due to cultural conditioning and shaming, and outdated beliefs regarding what constitutes healthy emotional expression. It is a beautiful thing to experience the perspective of an in-touch, connected man who feels safe to express his emotions freely. Thank you, Bradley Morris, for opening the door to this incredible way of moving through the experience of losing a loved one.

Be a man and cry like a baby

shared by Bradley Morris

"As I write this, my heart feels heavy and happy, sad and grateful.

My wife, Celeste, and I have made the decision to lay our loyal companion of 14 years, Sasha the dog, to rest next weekend (04/04-2015). It's so hard to believe because six weeks ago she was golfing with me every day, going for hikes and ripping it up in the forest like a young pup. That is, until a bad case of Vestibular syndrome hit her hard.

Today we spent the day present with our tears and each other. It is bittersweet knowing that we have these final seven days with Sasha before we will send her home.

The well of grief I'm present to is incredible and so beautiful. I'm grateful to be feeling this pain in my heart. It is a sign that my heart has swelled up with so much love that the only thing it could do is crack open and overflow with tears.

If it weren't for my wife, Celeste, I don't think I ever could've written what you are reading. So thank you, darling, for inspiring and teaching me so much about my own heart and emotions.

It wasn't until Celeste's father took his own life that I truly understood the full rainbow spectrum of emotions that are available and necessary for us to experience on our human journey. For two years (and a bit), I supported Celeste through a journey of deep grieving. At times I wondered if she'd ever come through the other side, but the spark of light in her eyes assured me that she would.

Being a man, I at first thought I could help fix her pain and sorrows; somehow make them right. But as time wore on and I watched her move through wave after wave of this tsunami of grief, I began to understand that there was nothing wrong. In fact, it was so perfect and right.

The grief she was feeling was a celebration, just like the grief that is spilling over from my heart right now is also a celebration for how much I love this beautiful being who has brought so much joy to our lives.

Witnessing Celeste embrace her own sadness, depression, tears and pain gave me permission to explore my own. In the last few years, I too have ridden many of my own waves, but I don't think any have been as big as the ones I'm feeling now.

Growing up in a culture where it's wrong for men to cry or to show any emotion other than anger, rage or happiness makes it challenging to be authentic. When we go to a funeral, we look around and see men wearing black sunglasses because they're afraid to show that they feel pain. They think it's weak.

How can it be weak for a man to love? Why is it that we praise men who do not feel? If we lived in a world where men were encouraged to feel their sorrows and share their emotions openly, I do believe we'd have less war, hatred and violence.

But instead we numb it with drugs and alcohol, we feel ashamed and wonder why we're not stronger, or we push it down and let it rot in our guts until it becomes rage that we often take out on others.

This idea that is so deeply ingrained in us is so ass-backwards. A man (or woman) who does not truly feel all of his emotions shuts his heart down, becomes bitter, rigid, angry and numb. This is not a man. This is not noble or honourable. It is cowardly.

For so many years, I wore a mask that I didn't even know I had on. I showed a fake smile to the world because that's what I thought I must do if I wished to be accepted or liked. I was so afraid to show my true colours, what was really present on the inside.

My invitation to my brothers of all ages is to be courageous and cry like a baby. Please show yourself to the world. Let yourself be vulnerable, because it is in breaking down that we build ourselves up to be stronger, more whole and more powerful.

There is no shame in being sad. There is nothing wrong, even when we feel that we might drown in the waves of grief that are crashing down on us. This is life. Celebrate the experience. Let the tears flow and, please, if there is someone you care about deeply in your life, let them know. Show them. Get off your computer and hold them. Because soon they may not be here and, unfortunately, we're not all fortunate to know the number of days we have left with those special someones in our life.

This is the bitter sweetness I am feeling right now. The gratitude that I still have seven days to cherish the touch of my sweet dog, Sasha, and the sadness of knowing that after that she will leave this beautiful world and return to where we all must go someday."

~ ~ ~

What a gift to be able to share with you now this powerful contribution from Bradley's wife and partner, **Celeste Morris**, honouring the many things she learned from the passing of her longtime companion and dearest friend, Sasha. Tissues recommended.

The Things I've Learned From My Dying Dog

shared by Celeste Morris

"Oh Sasha, Sasha, Sasha... Little Sasha Bear, my Boo, Bub, Bubba, BoobieDoo, Sashi, My Little Bugli, My Love... I miss you so.

It's been a few months now since you've departed this place, and my heart aches with deep joy and sadness for knowing you and missing you.

I know you are happy up there, wherever you are, being all infinite and aglow without limitations.

I feel you here sometimes, surrounding me. I know you come to be with me. I can feel your comforting energy like a cozy blanket some days.

You remind me, when I forget, that you aren't gone, that you are here and everywhere, and in fact only a finger's breadth away. I miss stroking your fur, and petting your belly, and seeing your ears flap in the wind out the car window. I miss your bouncy trot and fluffy tail on walks, and how you ran around all crazy on the trails some days when you were hyper. I miss how attentive you became at mealtime and the joy of sharing food and snuggles with you. Oh the snuggles... our cozy morning snuggles, nothing in the world could compare.

122

When you got sick I felt devastated beyond repair; cracked completely wide open. As though I were thrust all the way through a threshold into a land that belongs solely to Source embodied, a place where all that matters is breath and the simplicity of being in the moment.

It's funny, because even in this place of grace, I remember sobbing uncontrollably on your bed, completely turned over to the wretched aching love and sorrow, begging for your pardon. I knew the best thing I could do to support you was to remain calm, grounded and centred, but I just couldn't. I lost all control.

You have crawled so far into my heart, and the imminence of your departure rattled and shook my heart open to breaking point as you danced and leapt out toward a new kind of freedom.

In your life, you saturated me with a love so pure, a love I had never experienced before I knew you. It shook me to my core to see you in pain, to watch helplessly as you suffered. Your bravery was exceptional, and your courage inspiring. You gave me strength and coached me through your illness even while you rested.

It was the most exquisite thing, to be with you in presence during the last days of your life. I learned so much about being present and in the moment, like truly in the moment with you. I learned what it is to lovingly be of service to your highest will and support you through your choice to leave. I learned that no matter what happens in life, we are incredibly gifted in the simplicity of good food, clean water to drink, a safe place to be still, and the comfort of family and friends.

You have selflessly gifted me countless beautiful memories, shared your regal wisdom and offered your healing ways to support me over our 13 years together.

In fact, you taught me so much in our final days together that I wrote a list to remember them. So thank you, my sweet darling Sasha. It's the highest honour to be your kindred.

1. Be in the Moment. I know, it's so zen. You're welcome.

2. During a time of tragedy, illness, grieving, or dying, it can be very helpful and confirming to have an outside neutral perspective. Someone to facilitate a 'check in' on behalf of you or a loved one to get a read on what's really going on and what is needed in an optimal way. Traumatic shock can cloud our ability to hear what messages our body and life are leading us to see, and it can be so valuable to have somebody with an outside perspective provide you with some clarity in a time of crisis.

3. That being said, the most personal decisions need to be made from the depth of your own heart. Some decisions should not be overly influenced or made by an outside source. No one can provide the same barometer as your own heart. A person outside of oneself can provide a container and space to find that inner reflection, but it's ultimately our choices and our decisions that matter.

Sometimes we need the help of others to see what is really inside us all along.

4. Which is sort of my round-a-bout way of saying that the hardest decisions in life are yours, and yours alone to make. We need to feel confident and at peace with our choices, so maintaining our personal power and exercising our will to choose is an important aspect of difficult life decisions. It needs to be an inner journey that you perform on your own or with your family involved to receive this type of information as confirmation that this decision comes from you, rather than from an outside source. It's all about going within and seeking the answers from the heart.

5. Respect the choices of others, period. When our dog decided she was ready to go, I got behind her decision 100%. That is the way I speak my love to her—by being supportive of her will. Only she truly knows what is best for her. When I understand this and claim that same lesson for myself, I am more easily able to extend that to others.

6. Dying is the most natural thing in the world. It's as natural as dancing and singing and smiling and eating and loving. It's a part of the whole picture of life.

7. Food is really awesome. It's a gift. Cherish it.

8. It's okay to ask for help for yourself and for others. Sasha had this beautiful way of gathering people together. When she became ill, we enlisted the support of our community, who showed up for us in the most beau-

tiful of ways. This was incredibly profound for me to surrender to what was being asked of me in each moment, knowing we were supported.

9. When the tears flow, let 'em rock! It's totally normal to let the expression of love out through your tears. You might set off other people's sprinkler system, and that's OK too. They probably needed the release. I still release my hot salty tears like a badge of honour when the waves come. It's part of how I praise you and express my love.

10. You can be Happy and Grieving at the same time. Yes, you heard that right. It's entirely possible to be weeping with grief and happy in your heart at the same exact moment. Cherish the gift of loving by allowing the nature of grief to grace your heart too.

11. Lying in the grass is heaven to a dog. So take time just to lay in the grass, which brings us back to #1, 'Be in the Moment'."

~ ~ ~

Thank you, Celeste and Bradley, for allowing me to share here what is in your hearts. And thank you, Sasha, for your incredible contribution to the lives of so many.

Our animals have the potential to take us to deep, amazing places if we allow them to. Often, we share a profound love with them and let them deeper into our hearts than any human. Our grief over their passing from our lives is natural and essential. How we grieve, how we move through this process and find our way to the other side, is perfect. Know that there will always be a middle—the messy, deeply uncomfortable place where we feel most in the darkness. Honour it and allow it, trusting that it means you're moving closer to the light at the end of the tunnel. Give yourself the space to be with all of it. And if you need a helping hand and guide through your process, as we all do, reach out to Celeste or someone like her. It is not a journey that is meant to be made alone.

The space in the middle

Taking time and space to grieve may sound like a relatively simple task. Ideally, we'll block it out in our calendar, taking the time we need and reserving the space to cry, to fall apart, to deeply feel the loss of a beloved and to slowly find our peace and resolution. The reality is that the many moving parts of our life can easily sidetrack us and our need for space, especially when that space is specifically for feelings—some rather uncomfortable feelings. Holding the space to feel and grieve the loss of our animal fully and completely is not for the meek at heart. But, there is a downside or two to filling up all our much-needed processing space with other activities.

The new age term for this is bypassing. And we do it all the time, more often than not without even knowing it.

Here's why it's a big deal. If we think of life as a place to learn a thing or two, then bypassing, or jam-packing our processing space with activities and "stuff," is like skipping school. It is an avoidance strategy, and a successful one at that, used effectively to allow us to not really deal with what needs to be dealt with. We are experts at stuffing, skimming over and moving on, skills learned early on to avoid conflict and avert discomfort and pain. There is not a single human in existence who doesn't do this. After all, it's an impressively effective way to not really feel the sucky stuff.

Here's the issue. All that sucky stuff just gets put aside for later, making our next similar-feeling experience that much more excruciating. It's like putting down a huge fishing net when all we want is one fish. We're going to get a whole lot more than we bargained for, including everything that the unconscious mind relates to that one fish. So in the case of our animal moving through their final transition, we might experience all of the grief that is left unprocessed from the deaths of all the loved ones who have already passed over, along with any fear in our subconscious about our own death. And to describe it as overwhelming is an understatement when this barrage of emotions hits home. Eventually, avoidance is no longer a strategy, when either the physical body starts showing evidence of the stress of unprocessed stuff, or the mind can no longer contain the overflow. Deep down we always know that this tactic is not a long-term solution and that something has to give, which brings me back to the need for taking space.

Let me be blunt. Take space. Even if it feels selfish or over-the-top. Even if people try to tell you, "It's just a dog/horse/cat," and even if your life doesn't seem to permit it, I strongly encourage you to do whatever it takes to create the space you need. Maybe it's only for a few days. Maybe it means putting yourself on a plane to somewhere half a world away, sitting on a remote beach and letting the ocean and the palm trees soothe your soul and nurture your heart. Maybe it means healing or counseling sessions once a week for six months. Or a wellness workshop. Or yoga. Or journaling. Or just breathing. Or meditation. Or retreating from the world and drawing long baths and crying for hours. Or calling a friend who gets what you're moving through and having a meaningful conversation. Taking space is going to look unique for each person and each situation.

Beware of the space-fillers and the well-disguised feeling-avoidance strategies. The "I'll just head out on a vacation and work the entire time." Or the "I'll take this long bath and read romance novels." Or the classic, "Maybe I just need to fill this very uncomfortable void with _____ and I'll feel way better." The truth is that with these strategies you rarely feel better in the long run, even if things seem better for a few moments or a few days. Ask yourself honestly, "Am I allowing myself the space to feel and to grieve?" Yes, feeling our feelings really sucks sometimes. It hurts. It makes sense that we avoid them and deny them. And processing the death of a loved one fully can feel so, so hard. There's really no way to dress it up. But when we can and do allow ourselves the space and time to feel, life gets a whole lot better for us and for our animals. The reality is we can't skip the messy middle—it is an essential step in the process of healing and finding resolution.

In a few chapters, I'll be mapping out some strategies to help you and your animals move through their final transition and beyond as gracefully as possible. Some of these strategies and techniques assume that the passing of your pet is due to old age. It's essential to address the process of aging, something I've learned about from hundreds of clients and, more personally, from my whippet, B, who passed on just over two years ago at 16 years of age. And we also need to address the very different experience of navigating an abrupt transition, a tragic or unexpected end, which can be even harder to swallow. As much as we try to prepare for the inevitable, there are some things that are impossible to prepare for.

When tragedy strikes

Let's spend a moment talking about shock and trauma. Both of these can affect us deeply and profoundly, leaving emotional and physical scars that can last a lifetime. When we experience a shock, the effect on the body and mind can range from minor to devastating. I could include some real life examples here, but I think we're all probably good without one more tragic story raining on our parade at the moment. I'm also sure we can all get the picture from personal experience. There are few beings walking this earth that are untouched by shock, trauma or tragedy of some nature.

Suffice it to say that an abrupt and unexpected ending to the life of a loved one can leave a substantial and lasting mark. With little or no time to process our feelings or even say goodbye, this type of death can be difficult (if not impossible) to swallow, much less digest. It means that our goodbyes and our "I wish I had's" come after the fact. And it means that we are often left to process not only our grief, but also an intense combination of anger, shock, guilt and fear all at the same time. Our brains and hearts are attempting to deal with the fact that a key player in our life is now gone, a change that is almost impossible to fathom and even more difficult to process with any sort of clarity. In this type of situation, to say we feel overwhelmed is very much an understatement.

Remember, first and foremost, that your experience is always valid, whatever it is. Death sucks, no matter how it happens or how long you have to prepare. And if you have experienced a tragic sudden death, you know first-hand that this takes the cake when it comes to the sheer suckiness of it all. That is why I want to talk about some ways to make this experience just a little more bearable.

I was once called out to work with a horse who had accidentally broken her leg running through her paddock. In the horse world, a broken leg is equivalent to a death sentence, due to the amount of weight that the leg would be required to bear, making healing impossible. When I arrived, her herd was gathered around her; the vet had made the decision to put her down and she was already gone, a large sheet pulled over her still figure. Her owner was beside herself with grief, and it was obvious that her equine companions were in shock. When I began to communicate with the soul or spirit of this horse, it was clear she too was in shock, taken very much by surprise by the dramatic turn of events. The session, one of my most memorable to date, was focused on helping her make her final transition easily and with understanding, helping her herd mates process the shock and grief arising over her sudden parting and adjust to the new herd dynamic, and helping her person find her way through her overwhelming grief and incomprehension of this traumatic change. The hour I spent with this small connected herd was filled with release after release as the energetics were re-calibrated and we addressed the shock waves, both emotional, energetic and spiritual, of such an event. Afterwards, the horses stayed with the body of their herd mate for hours, continuing their grieving process. I felt so blessed to be even a small part of relieving the trauma and shock intertwined in this unexpected event and to share in the resulting and equally unexpected feeling of peace.

If you have experienced the sudden, unexpected death of a loved one and are still feeling the fallout of shock and trauma, know that you are not alone. You are not alone in feeling countless powerful emotions and deep, seemingly unbearable wounding around this event. Remember, this was not just a dog/horse/cat; this was a beloved and irreplaceable member of your family, a shoulder to cry on, a dear friend and a trusted confidant. The deep grief and feelings of pain and loss you are experiencing are not only merited, but natural. There is every possibility that you will need substantial time and space for your healing process and that it will be messy, emotional and as individual as you are. Remember that time will heal most of your wounds, but it may not heal all of them. It is very likely that you will need support to help you through your unique process of resolution.

We are blessed to have some incredible, trustworthy healing practitioners in our world who are able to hold the space for you to find resolution and, eventually, peace. When you are ready, consider making an appointment with someone you trust (referrals from friends are a great place to start) and consider that appointment and any down the road as a commitment to the long-term well-being of your heart, your body, your mind, your family and your life. You'll be blown away by how free you feel when you release the trauma and shock of this event, which are often stored deep down in your cells.

Combining this commitment to our own healing with our own unique way of honouring our animal can help our bruised and broken heart to slowly, but surely, find healing. For all who have lost a loved one, no matter the cause, part of the resolution comes through ritual and reverence. When we take the space and time to honour the life and the passing of our beloved animals in our own unique way, we find an incredible amount of peace and understanding. Be sure to read on—the coming pages are all about creating rituals, a beautiful and poignant way to support both you and your animals in moving through the loss of a dear friend.

Resolution through ritual

Around the world, final transitions are accompanied by countless traditions, rituals and ceremony. You could argue that some of these processes are more effective than others, that some dive deeper, bring more honour, and hold more space. Good thing we're doing things differently around here. Because in this book, as you might have noticed, we're not dealing in concrete, "right" ways to do anything. Instead, the priority is on what feels good and right for you. Yes, it's true. I'm a rebel with a cause. I think that being preachy about anything sucks, mainly because I believe that in each one of us is an innate knowing of what is right and true for us in each moment. And yes, now I have to go back through everything and make sure I'm not being a complete hypocrite. Which is entirely possible. And if so, I apologize. The fact is I really have no clue what is perfect for you, so I'm not even going to attempt to tell you what that is.

And so, anything goes when it comes to your unique ritual for your unique animal. I remember as a kid having a pet cemetery in our backyard and creating rituals to say goodbye to our various hamsters and guinea pigs, including an honouring speech, tears shed, a small handmade, decorated cross, and flowers. With my whippet, B, my goodbyes were said in the months before her passing, our final ritual more energetic than physical. I felt her joy and release in leaving her aging and increasingly limited physical shell, and watched her in my mind's eye with amazement and disbelief as she walked between two rows of bowing and reverent animals on her return to the beyond. She was buried with love with the help of a friend under the fir trees and the eagles, wrapped in her favourite blanket and covered in flowers, while we reminisced and shared story after story of her fabulous 16-year walk on Earth. Afterwards, I shared my love and gratitude for her with my community—the stories that were shared about how she had touched so many lives are something I will treasure for a long time to come. Another client, upon a prompting by her passing German Sheppard who was deeply connected to her family as a protector and caretaker, wrote a poem and created a beautiful plaque with a photo to hang in a place of honour. Others still choose cremation, weaving the ashes of their loved one into beautiful objects and spreading them where their animal found their joy.

No need to get bogged down by the common definition of ritual here. In many dictionaries, it is defined as a customary set of steps performed according to a prescribed order. You're in rebel territory now, so I hope you don't mind if we throw that particular definition right out the window. I want the steps that you take to feel good, healing, and right for you, no matter what everyone else is doing. And if they feel good for others too, which is more than likely the case, bonus! Be creative, be intuitive and follow your feel-good feelings to a ritual that feels just right for you and your animal. Ask for help, both externally and intuitively, if you are having trouble connecting to what this looks like for you (are you noticing a trend here?). The only necessities are that your ritual addresses these key aspects, and even these are open to interpretation.

1) *Reverence and Honouring*

A ritual is an opportunity to express our reverence for this beautiful being, the gifts they brought to our life, and what they have shared with us and others. This may look like a moment of silence and connection, a prayer, a poem, a blessing, an offering of sacred stones, flower petals, herbs or cherished-memory items (like a collar, special tag or brush). We may also feel called to light a candle, wrap our animal in their favourite blanket (if they are still with us in physical presence), or even dance or sing in their honour. If we decide to cremate our animal, we may feel inspired to spread their ashes in their favourite spot or sprinkle them in a space in nature where we can go to sit and contemplate.

2) *Sharing and Gratitude*

Whether we share the space with others who feel the love or move through our ritual solo, the main thing is to share our feelings and depth of gratitude to our animal for their time in our life. I invite you to create a scrapbook or start a new journal. Write down your feelings and memories, add pictures, share your love and gratitude for them with your trusted community, or find a poem or passage that fits for you and your animal and speaks to your heart and to theirs. Share what you loved about them and how they made your life better. This is an opportunity to say thank you for everything you have received and to open up to the gifts they have brought you during your time together. This step is definitely going to need tissues.

3) *Releasing and Integration*

This is the hardest part—releasing your grip on what was, and accepting what is. Take the time in your ritual, as long as it takes (moments, days, even months or years, in some cases), to gradually let go and release your animal to the next steps of their journey, wherever they may be. This part may require support from someone who can help you and your animal to fully complete the transition and understand the depth of your connection with them in the past, present and as you move into the future. The process will be unique for each animal and each partnership, and it is a creative one—there are no rules about how it should look, how long it should last or what you should do. As I mentioned, one of my clients wrote a poem about her dog, which she transformed into a plaque with her picture. This process allowed her to integrate her experience with her dog and understand more deeply the role she played in her life, leading to even more gratitude and reverence. Another client took her beloved canine's ashes to her favourite hiking spot to be scattered. In a powerful honouring process in our first Death Sucks workshop, one animal lover was able to connect with her dog who had passed on 18 years ago and understand the true nature of their connection - in essence, she was finally able to unwrap the gift her animal had given her so many years ago. In doing so, she could feel a sense of this leg of the journey coming to completion and an exciting new time beginning.

Take the time to create a unique ritual that will help you begin the process of releasing, understanding and fully integrating what you feel, what you have learned and how you have been transformed by this powerful connection. You'll be amazed how much this one part of the process can ease your heart and bring you the resolution and peace you seek.

Grief is not something we find an end to or wake up one day to discover that it is gone for good. Grief, at its essence, is one of the most potent forms of love. It means we are feeling, loving beings, with a capacity for the deepest love and connection. Just like the ocean, the waves of our grief will continue to ebb and flow for our entire existence, with days of total calm and days of utter chaos. Our only role here is to be with the grief that arises, to acknowledge it and be real with it, and to let it roll through. I grant you every permission to be as messy as necessary—realness is essential to resolution and to growth. Let the tears flow and the mucous pour forth, let the mascara run and the wailing emerge—this is how we honour the love that we have shared and how we find our way back to wholeheartedness and profound connection.

And God asked the feline spirit
"Are you ready to come home?"

"Oh, yes, quite so," replied the precious soul.
"And as a cat, you know I am most able to decide anything for myself."

"Are you coming then?" asked God.
"Soon," replied the whiskered angel.
"But I must come slowly
My human friends are troubled
For you see, they need me, quite certainly."

"But don't they understand?" asked God –
"That you'll never leave them?
That your souls are intertwined, for all eternity,
That nothing is created or destroyed,
It just is . . . forever and ever and ever?"

"Eventually they will understand," replied the cat.
"For I will "Whisper" in her heart – that I am always with
her.
I just am . . . forever and ever and ever!"

– Unknown

Chapter 6

Committing for the long haul

One of my biggest lessons from the animals in my life is also a deeply humbling one. It is the lesson of commitment. In my decade of working with thousands of animals and their people, I have seen the same thing over and over again and it continues to amaze and inspire me. And sometimes, it just brings me to my knees with awe. Animals seem to innately know who they are meant to commit to, what to teach and learn, and when to let go and make their final transition.

When my mare, Diva, came into my life 12 years ago, after four deals to buy her fell through in one way or another, it felt like I had been hit by cupid's arrow, or something like it. I was struck, perhaps most deeply, by the experience of a deep spiritual and emotional connection, something I had no previous frame of reference for understanding. With the help of my mentor at the time, I committed verbally to Diva, staring her in the eyes and letting her know that she would be in my life and by my side until (and yes, I did put it this eloquently) one of us bit it.

The first years of our relationship were devastatingly hard, a fight, but our connection planted roots for a commitment that went beyond comfort or whether she was behaving like a good horse (most of the time in those early years, she was not). But the truth is that I was not really behaving like a great human either—that was the truly humbling bit, the part that was tortuously hard to swallow. That, more than anything, was my commitment: to do my own work, to move through my own patterns and old paradigms, to show up with more and more congruency and realness in our interactions. Now, 12 years later, these besties in different bodies have one of the most awesome partnerships around, in my very biased opinion. And a big part of that is the commitment to navigating everything this journey has put on our path. As I shared earlier, one of the reasons I wrote this book is to prepare for the inevitable passing of my best friend, my beautiful, magical horse. I want to stand by her side powerfully, to show up for her with my whole heart as she makes her final transition as my partner, something that will take more courage, commitment and grace than anything I have faced yet.

It is impossible to discern, with Diva and my other animals, whether I chose them or they chose me. I have come to accept that it is equal measures of both, and there are bigger reasons for walking this path together. Not long after Diva and I found each other, an animal communicator shared that we had come to this Earth at this time to show others the beautiful possibility of being best friends in different bodies. That idea has stayed with me and informed my decisions and understanding ever since—a reminder that there is so much more at work than meets the eye. Animals seem to understand that the more access we have to our deeper knowing and intuition, the easier it is to make a commitment to ourselves, to our lives and to what inspires us. It is inspiring to watch how they commit deeply to us, forgiving us over and again, showering us with love when we need it and always showing us exactly what we need to see.

I bring up commitment here because during our pet's final transition, this essential aspect becomes even more relevant. The aging process can be a challenging one, not just for our animals, but for us. It is often accompanied by many changes, some not as welcome or as easy to swallow as others. It is a time that can test our patience and our ability to stay committed and connected, as we navigate the inherent challenges that accompany this process. My beautiful, sweet whippet, B, was a great example.

She turned 16 on Oct 26, 2012 and passed on peacefully about six months later. B entered my life at the age of nine, a miraculous and incredible addition to my existence. She was one of those animals who touched every human being in her vicinity, with a spirit as large as a house, and a softness and dedication that only sighthound lovers might understand. In her final two years, she was all but deaf, her breath could knock someone out from three feet away, despite missing a number of teeth and my then continuous brushing, she was experiencing varying degrees of cognitive dysfunction and, perhaps most challenging, she had a long-time habit of peeing in the house. From the very beginning of our relationship, when she arrived in my life quite magically at 9 years old, B would communicate her stress, particularly her anxiety around being left alone for any amount of time, through accidents on the floor. This shifted to peeing on bedding, couches and, in her final, most confused months, even on me.

I willingly admit there was a part of me that took this behaviour very personally. Through much breathing and even more inner soul-searching and healing work, I recognized that B's behaviour was asking me for a new and deeper level of commitment to our relationship. It also challenged me to be even more accepting and loving in the difficult moments. In the end, the commitment to my own work, and the subsequent balance that it brought to our relationship, meant we spent the final months of her Earth walk in harmony and connection. And I learned a thing or two about how to be present and deeply loving to another being, despite challenges. What a gift.

Animals, being some of our greatest teachers, often play a role in shining a light on the parts of ourselves we have buried or attempted to deny. The value of looking deeply into these shadowy places is priceless to our development and discovery of self. And in situations such as my journey with B, they teach us how to stay with something even when it's uncomfortable and our initial inclination is to flee, to take it personally, to get angry or to hide.

In the work of self-discovery, it is important to understand that when we feel uncomfortable with or resistant to something, it is often an area that holds opportunity for great learning about ourselves. Death is definitely one such experience. It is rare to find a person who feels totally comfortable with death and dying, especially when they are navigating the impending death of a beloved animal companion. It can be difficult to stay present and available when we experience this depth of discomfort. Using the tools we've already worked with, including the breath and allowing ourselves to feel and express, we can move in a healthy way through our emotions, rather than avoiding or denying them. Emotion is energy moving. So when the breath is used effectively, it is able to move and release the emotions that are arising.

A core message in all of this is one that author Brené Brown speaks to beautifully in her new book, *Rising Strong* (which is a must-read, by the way!). She explains that you can't skip the messy middle—that place where there is no going back, and the way forward is still dark and murky. This place, uncomfortable as it may be, is an essential part of the journey. So it is in life and in death— this messy middle is the place where "what is" is making way for what is meant to be, an excruciating pause before resolution. And we never know quite how long it's going to last, so most of us prefer to fill this space with anything else but this terrifyingly messy, emotional and unpredictable experience. Our movement through the experience of losing a loved one contains this scary essential step—it is present in every transformative and challenging experience of our lives.

Committing to staying present for your animals can be an incredible way for both of you to move through this transition with more grace and ease. This may mean long, messy nights and lots of tissues. Processing all of this emotion allows us to reap the benefits of wisdom that we are building from our experience in the world and with our animals. I like to think of it as panning for emotional gold, also known as wisdom. By releasing blocks to feeling, integrating our experience and allowing energy to flow, we can be more connected to our animals, to ourselves, and to our lives, a very beautiful side-effect.

Mercy as love

On the topic of commitment, and with the understanding that we are the stewards of our animals, I want to briefly address the sometimes touchy topic of euthanasia. Offering our animals relief from suffering is, in my mind, one of the greatest gifts we can give them. In my experience, it is rare that a domesticated animal completes their final transition peacefully on their own. Although it does happen occasionally, it is far more common for an animal to struggle to hang on, despite their level of suffering. In the wild, an animal suffering in this way is often put out of their misery by a nearby predator, but in the case of domestication, we often find ourselves in the position of having to make the final call. What I have experienced time and time again is that many animals will hang on until the bitter end, enduring a great deal of suffering and discomfort. The body is an incredibly resilient machine, sometimes a little too resilient, one could argue. This means that, as our animal's steward, it is often up to us to make a decision for our animal about the timing of their passing.

A few things are necessary in this area. The first is a team that you trust, including a veterinarian who is not afraid to share the honest truth about your animal's condition and all of your options, if any. The second is to take the time now to strengthen your connection, especially on the subtle, intuitive level, with your animal. This will give you the capacity to "read" your animal's levels of discomfort and their readiness to make their transition. If you feel unable to connect or get a read in this area, consider bringing in a trusted professional skilled in animal communication or intuitive work to help you find clarity. The third is to show mercy through letting go. That may look like giving your animal verbal permission to make their final transition, especially if they have held an essential job in your family for your time together, as is the case with many dogs and horses. Sharing your gratitude for a job extremely well done and coming to a place of allowing them to go are both important steps in this process.

This is a time to put aside your own desires and truly step into the role of steward for your animal. The hard-to-swallow reality is that what they need might be completely opposite to what you are wanting, especially if they are ready to transition and you don't want them to go. Keep coming back to the question "What is best for them?" Take a deep breath and move forward with love in your heart and trusted support by your side.

From personal experience, I know that if the time is right and your animal is ready to make their transition, a veterinarian-assisted passing is typically an incredibly peaceful event, especially if a sedative is used during the process. My highest recommendation would be to work with a veterinarian who is able to come to your home, if this service is available in your area, to ensure the greatest amount of relaxation and the space and freedom to grieve the loss of a beloved family member.

When staying is painful

Let's extend this discussion about commitment a little bit further and broach the topic of one of the greatest challenges to our commitment. By far, one of the most uncomfortable things for any animal lover is to see their animals suffer. And because of our "stuff" around death, we equate those final moments, those last few breaths, with the most suffering. Whether this is true or not is irrelevant. For some animals, perhaps it is, but for most, it is not.

The fact of the matter is that many people aren't there beside their animals in those last moments because of their own discomfort around their pet's perceived suffering. And this absence has the effect of making these final moments unnecessarily anxiety-ridden and upsetting for our animals. Yes, I am about to get preachy, even though I promised not to. This is not about guilting or shaming, but it is a reality check. If you feel incapable of spending the last moments of your animal's life in their presence, I ask you to put yourself in their paws for a moment. Imagine spending your life with a family and then, at the time of your final transition, being dropped off with strangers or, worse yet, people you don't like or trust, to take your last breaths. Imagine the stress levels rising when you realize you have to travel this uncharted territory with no familiar faces, no comforting voices. I'm not going to sugar coat it—it would flat-out suck. When we commit to our animals, part of this involves traversing the places that don't feel good or comfortable because we love them and we are their stewards. Holding space for them during this time, providing comfort and unconditional love as their spirit passes from their bodies, is one of the greatest gifts we can give them and ourselves.

If you find being present for your animal at this time overwhelming or impossible, do what it takes to shift your experience. Get the help you need, clear the fears that need to be cleared, release everything that is getting in the way. If you just can't make it work due to timing or something impossible to shift, make sure a loved one who is close to your pet is there by their side. There are many health and wellness professionals who can help you move through your resistance and into a place of more openness, acceptance and empathy. This moment, this sacred and challenging moment, holds closure, beauty and transformation—and is absolutely meant to be shared. What can you do to ensure you'll be there?

Chapter 7

Tools in your tool kit

As a health practitioner and a human being, it became pretty clear to me early on in my healing journey that I needed to put some handy tools in my tool kit for navigating life's inevitable twists and turns. By tools, I mean healing modalities, information, wisdom, tidbits, books, videos and anything else that I found to be in any way helpful. As you can imagine, almost 12 years later, my tool box is pretty full, especially with my seemingly insatiable appetite for new information and skills. I love using my tools, polishing them, sharing them with others and, of course, having them around just in case. The number of times they have come in handy just for my small animal family is remarkable. They have also been pivotal in my development as what I refer to as a helpful human being. Before I began acquiring these tools, life was very different. I was not a particularly balanced or happy individual—quite the opposite actually.

My strategy for handling death and dying prior to the development of my well-being tool kit looked a little like this: cry incessantly for many days, feel everyone else's emotions, cry for them, attempt to stuff my emotion, feel lost and separate, sit in my room alone and cry, and then cry afterwards at anything that would remind me of the deceased. And even after all of that, I would still feel shut-down and disconnected rather than relieved. My grandma's passing was a prime example of this pattern. She died tragically when I was 14 and long before I had any understanding of what it meant to be a highly sensitive empath and that I was one. This was also the case with my hamster, Squeaky, who passed on when I was 10 years old.

My response to loss after the development of my handy tool kit looked quite different. When my grandfather passed on, I was able to help him with his transition using energy medicine. I felt a healthy connection to him and still do. I cried prior to and at his funeral, releasing any unprocessed emotions, but not sponging the emotions of anyone else in the room. I felt a sense of spaciousness, freedom and peace as I connected energetically with the journey of his spirit leaving his exhausted physical form. What a relief this new experience of death and dying was!

What I've realized after working with thousands of clients is that offering people empowering tools is one way to spread the healing and good stuff around. It's one thing to go to a practitioner to for help healing yourself and your animals, and quite another to feel empowered to help yourself. That being said, surrounding yourself with a great support team is absolutely essential at any stage of your journey with your animal(s). But there is something incredible about having a few great tools at your fingertips—you can choose the team you want to have and know when you need their help!

Building our own tool kit can feel like a big leap because trusting ourselves and our own skill set can take time. Plus, we're well-trained to not get "too big for our britches" and to leave things like this to the "experts." After watching many people venture into tool kit building, I can assure you that you are capable of great things, including learning how to help yourself and others. Your specific combination of skills will be different from mine or anyone else's, comprised of all the wisdom from your past experience and the learning you have done in your life, plus whatever you want to add in.

Alright, let's dive in! Here's a few great tools that you can easily add to your tool kit to help make the final transition of your companion animals easier for everybody concerned.

Flower Power

First up is one of my absolute favourite additions to my tool kit: vibrational remedies. I started using vibrational remedies, otherwise known as flower essences, as a way to work with some of the deeper stuff affecting well-being, namely the emotional and spiritual components. At the time, I found I was only getting so far with purely physical bodywork and needed a little help getting under the surface. And that's exactly what these powerful remedies did! Countless times my mind was blown by their potency and effectiveness, and it continues to be even now, many years later. Here's the story of Smokey the cat and how vibrational remedies helped her.

Smokey was a different sort of cat. The details of her past were unclear, but one can only guess that she had been mistreated. Her home and person were supportive and loving, but until we started working with flower remedies, she found comfort and safety in one small space: Smokey lived in the bathroom cupboard. My first session with Smokey, a beautiful tabby, was spent in an entirely separate room from her cramped abode. I communicated with her using Applied Kinesiology (AK), also known as muscle testing. I was able to work with her from the other room by using a surrogate to connect with her energy "field." Animals tend to feel very comfortable with Applied Kinesiology, and for one like Smokey, it can be the key to building trust in the practitioner and the process. We'll talk about this very cool technique in a little bit.

Although there were some improvements from her first session, her owner, Elaine, and I continued to search for something that would bring her out of her cupboard and into the light. In late November, during a session with Elaine, Smokey let us know through our intuitive work that a difficult spay had left her stressed, and physically and emotionally unbalanced. We understood from her that what she needed to correct this imbalance was one particular sea essence from Pacific Essences, a vibrational remedy company founded by my friend and colleague Sabina Pettitt and based on the west coast of Vancouver Island about an hour away from my home. The essence we used was barnacle, an incredible little sea creature that graces the rocky crags and tidal pools of our coastline. This essence is created using sea water collected from the direct vicinity of barnacles (don't worry, no barnacles were harmed in the making of this essence!). The vibration of this small sea creature focuses on supporting and healing the female aspect and the female reproductive system, a seemingly perfect match for the issue that Smokey had shared with us.

Several days later, I received an elated call from Elaine. Smokey had spent a good portion of the day in the common area of the house and had insisted on climbing under the covers in the bed to sleep. Elaine was overjoyed at the shift, which, even more amazingly, was last-

ing. This story is one of many demonstrating the sometimes miraculous effects of vibrational medicine. Because they work on a vibrational or energetic level,
flower and sea essences are incredibly effective when
used to balance any kind of emotional imbalances in
your pet. Anxiety, grief, fear and jealousy are just a few
of the emotions that these essences can help to bring
into balance.

So, you might be wondering, how are vibrational remedies made? It's actually quite a simple process, although
it requires an incredible depth of intuition and connection to nature to do it well. A flower essence is, essentially, an infusion of flowers in water. The flowers are
placed in a bowl of water in sunlight or moonlight; they
are then reverently discarded, leaving only the essence or
vibrational character of the flower. This infusion is then
mixed with a small amount of alcohol as a preservative.
For sea essences, sea water surrounding the creature is
used in the same way, preserving the vibration while doing no harm to the gracious being supporting us through
their unique energetic imprint. The gentleness of these
essences ensures gentle, albeit often very profound, healing—as was the case with Smokey. If the remedy is not
necessary, there will simply be no effect.

Many of you might be familiar with one of the most
powerful flower essences, a combination of five Bach
flower remedies called Rescue Remedy. It is an essential
in any first aid kit, perfect for dealing with shock, illness,

trauma or stress. Run, don't walk, to get this one into your medicine cabinet for you and your animals. It can work like magic, perfect for stressful or upsetting situations. It goes without saying that this is a remedy to have on hand to aid both you and your animal through their final transition. The tremendous healing properties of Rescue Remedy for both people and animals have been well documented worldwide.

The next big question: how do you take them? Administering flower essences is safe and easy. Two to three drops can be placed directly into your pet's mouth or into their drinking water, taking care not to contaminate the dropper or put yourself in danger of being bitten. If your animal dislikes the taste, dilute two drops of the remedy in a tablespoon of fresh spring water and use this new dilution as above. A two-drop dosage three to four times per day is recommended. Remember, it will take some time for the remedies to begin working effectively. Sometimes, if the chosen remedy is the right one, there can be an initial adverse reaction in your animal or in yourself as emotional and physical stagnancy begins to clear. This is, ironically, a positive sign that the remedy is a good fit for you, as it indicates things are moving and shaking. In this case, I encourage sticking with it for a little longer.

Pacific Essences (www.pacificessences.com) now makes specific animal flower essence blends for animals. These blends use vibration to create harmony, combining several remedies to create a combination that is effective for a specific situation or behaviour. Pacific Essences Co-founder Sabina Pettitt is not only a dear friend, but also an absolutely dedicated animal mom and a doctor of Traditional Chinese Medicine. Her essences and essence blends are some of the best I've ever worked with. I've used them extensively for the past eight years with amazing results. I also enjoy working with Bach Flower Essences, and there has been excellent research done on their positive effects for animals.

If your animal has some stuff happening that you can't seem to figure out, vibrational remedies might be your solution. A flower-essence specialist or Applied Kinesiologist can help you find the perfect essence. Or you may decide to develop your intuition by taking a course, learning Applied Kinesiology or developing your subtle senses through meditation or breath practice.

As luck would have it, I can help with this! How handy is that? Check out my online Applied Kinesiology for Animal Lovers course to learn this powerful tool and how to find the perfect essences for your unique animals. (http://bit.ly/kinetic-communication)

Kinetic Communication

This very cool tool is one that I use daily for myself, my animals and my clients. Each body has its own innate wisdom, or knowing of what it needs, and this tool is able to translate all of the communication from this innate wisdom and distill it into practical, usable information. My introduction to Applied Kinesiology, also known as muscle testing, came in Equine Sport Therapy School, where our head instructor Dave had been using this tool for a number of years to help horses and their riders, with miraculous results. I was initially resistant—I mean, could it really be possible to just simply ask the body what it needs and get an accurate response? It seemed almost too good to be true! It took me a good year and half of consistent use and consistent results to drop my doubts and finally trust myself. Happily, the majority of people are nowhere near as stubborn as I am, and I have been teaching courses in Applied Kinesiology for animals and their people for almost a decade now. It's one of those wellness tools that I firmly believe everyone should have in their tool kit.

So where did this muscle testing stuff come from? Applied Kinesiology (AK) as a scientific concept was developed in 1942 by Dr. George Goodhart. In his original experiments, he utilized a cybex dynamometer to determine changes in the amount of force developed with and without the addition of white sugar to the mouth of his subject. The decrease in force developed was so noticeable in his sugar-high subjects that he continued his research into this phenomenon for many years. The Touch for Health Method, developed by Dr. John Thie, carried on the tradition. This method connects the concept of AK with acupressure, the neurolymphatic system, the skeletal system, and the muscular system. Today, AK is used by health practitioners all over the world. It has practical applications in chiropractic medicine, aromatherapy, emotional balancing, acupressure and acupuncture, flower essences, nutrition, herbology, and countless other healing modalities.

And here's something even more cool. It is possible, effective, and very simple to use Applied Kinesiology with animals. I work with it as a form of simplified communication with my animal clients. Here is how it works: Basically, every body is made up of atoms and molecules, each with an electrical charge. The molecular structure of each carbon life form is unique, whether it be a human, an animal, or a tree. This electrical component is often referred to as the electromagnetic field, or sometimes as the aura. Just as magnets can be attracted to or repelled from each other, the electromagnetic fields of electrically charged objects can be compatible or incompatible. It is my understanding that in humans, animals, and many other life forms, the cellular memory or DNA imprint is found in our electromagnetic field. Essentially, AK can access this cellular memory to locate imbalances in the energetic body. In this way, it is incredibly useful in preventing illness or pain prior to manifestation in the physical body. It can locate imbalances in the energy field before they actually become physical imbalances. Illnesses or imbalances already manifesting in the physical body are often more difficult to work with and require more time and attention to heal properly.

So, how do you use AK with your animals? By using a surrogate to connect with the energy of the animal, it is possible to locate imbalances in your pet's physical, emotional, and spiritual systems. Animals tends to feel very comfortable with this type of work because they realize that they are being asked what is necessary for their unique system. Most animals I work with begin to trust the process within our first session together and are able to release pain, trauma, and stress, unravelling more layers as we get to know each other better and their trust builds. AK can also be used to determine the best course of action for each imbalance. For example, if a muscle is found to be weak, there are several methods of restoring strength, including energy work, massage, or pressure. The animal's body usually has a preference regarding the treatment method used. When clearing an emotional or spiritual imbalance, AK can help to uncover the root cause of the disharmony and reveal the best path to release the trauma.

One of my favourite things about Applied Kinesiology is the fact that anyone can easily learn and use this tool to help their animals or themselves. It is completely universal and is an amazing way to build trust in your intuitive skills, as an affirmation of your knowing. Plus, it pretty much feels like you're doing magic, which you kind of are. And that's just plain fun.

Start by working with the body pendulum exercise. I dare you to try this in the grocery store with some bananas or your favourite dessert.

Exercise: The Body Pendulum

Stand with your feet in a ballet position, heels together and toes pointed out. The purpose of this position is to put you slightly out of balance. You need to be a little bossy with your body before you begin—let it know that it can only sway forwards or backwards, not side to side.

Now close your eyes and ask your body to show you your "**yes**." Allow your body to sway forward or backward freely. Once you have a yes, ask your body to show you your "**no**." Again, allow your body to sway forward or backward freely. This should sway your body in the opposite direction. If there was little difference between your yes and your no, do this calibration process again, this time asking for a **stronger yes** and a **stronger no**.

Once you feel comfortable with these directions, test your reaction to different foods or nutritional supplements. You can do this by holding the substance up to your thymus gland, which is an energetically sensitive gland in the centre of the chest, directly under the sternum. If the substance is compatible with you, your body will sway to your **yes** position. If it is not compatible with your body, it will stay to the **no** position.

To test your animal using the body pendulum, picture your animal in your mind. This is the beginning of your Jedi training. Now, ask your body if you are testing your animal by using a simple statement. "I am testing _____(your animal's name)." Your body should sway to your **yes** position. If not, re-focus and try the question again. Once you have confirmed that you are working with your animal, the next step is asking permission. While thinking of your animal, ask the question "I have permission to work with _____ (animal's name here)." If the answer is yes, you've been given the all-clear to start testing! Re-do the calibration you did for yourself, this time finding out what your animal's yes and no feel like, as they might be quite different from yours. Once you feel confident in your calibration, you can start to test different foods and supplements for your animal by holding them up to your thymus gland. Remember, something is compatible if you move to the yes position, and not compatible if you move to the no position. For fun, compare your own test results for each supplement with the results of your animal. You'll be amazed at how often we are compatible with the same things as our animals, and vice versa!

Applied Kinesiology is a fabulous tool for the prevention of illness and maintaining and, most importantly, surpassing our expectations of health. It is also incredibly beneficial when it comes to navigating our animal's final transition, allowing us to be more connected with them, to develop our intuition and sense of timing and feel, and to establish a strong and supportive system of communication. It is easy to learn, quick and fun, and allows us to rapidly build a bridge of communication with our animal companion.

If you would like to learn more about this great tool, I have an online course that is fun, comprehensive and easy to follow. Learn more about it at this link —>
http://bit.ly/kinetic-communication)

I also teach this course in person and am in the process of developing additional trainings, including how to use Applied Kinesiology with flower essences, to balance the energy systems, to reduce discomfort and to increase mobility and circulation.

All about energy

We'll move on now to a set of powerful tools that is very near and dear to my heart. Over the last decade as an energy medicine practitioner, I've been blessed to see the amazing shifts possible for both animals and people with this type of work. I've also been blessed to have many colleagues who are at the cutting edge when it comes to working with energy. I've included my faves in this area in the Resources section at the back of the book.

So, what is energy work? Energy work operates from the belief that if we listen, the body can communicate to us exactly what is needed to heal itself. As you might have guessed, Applied Kinesiology and vibrational remedies both fit under this rather large umbrella. All forms of energy medicine, including Reiki, BodyTalk, Healing Touch, Emotional Freedom Technique and many, many more, work beautifully with animals. And one could argue that all forms of hands-on healing have a built-in energy work component. The reality is, down at our base level, we're made up of energy. For our animals, the healing methods that take into consideration their energetic foundation can support their healing process in an incredibly effective, gentle and often miraculous way. In the case of an animal's final transition, we are allowing their body-mind to co-ordinate whatever healing is a priority at that time. This might include building up the systems to allow the animal to live with greater quality for the remainder of their life or, in some cases, cultivating more ease, acceptance and relaxation throughout this inevitable transition.

The concept of energy medicine is simple: just get out of the way and allow the body and mind to do what they were designed to do—namely, balance and heal themselves. To think that we are even close to fully understanding the interconnectedness and pure genius of our bodies is unrealistic. There is so much cool stuff going on; it is safe to say that we have barely scratched the surface of what is possible!

Here's one great way to help you and your animals reduce stress, release tension and create clarity with the help of energy medicine. I've included a link below to a video of me teaching my fave brain balancing technique, (http://bit.ly/corticestechnique). In this video, I discuss how this quick and simple technique can work for you and your animals to calm the mind and positively influence everything from immune and digestive function to behaviour. It is also a powerful helper in emergency situations. I invite you to use this technique daily as a way to be pro-active about cultivating health and harmony. The more balanced your brain and body are now, the more you will be able to handle those stressful moments when they happen.

Journaling

When you're in the process of adding tools to your tool kit, journaling is one that is already there by default, just waiting to be discovered and explored. Why? Because anyone can do it with no more than a writing instrument and something to write on. Journaling can be as simple as drawing a picture in the sand or scribbling lines in your notebook that make no sense to anyone else. It can look like anything you want it to look like, making it a tremendously freeing experience for many.

The main purpose of journaling is to allow you to connect with, express and integrate what is going on inside. It can be a blissfully private affair, a place where you can share your secrets, open up deeply and vulnerably, and write expletive after expletive, if that's what feels right. Your journal will not take it personally if you yell in it, call it names or swear profusely. When it comes to huge transitions like death and dying, these forms of expression may be not only needed, but essential. As discussed earlier, resisting the expression of emotions can be damaging, and journaling provides a healthy, effective form of expression and integration. The feelings that arise are coming up to be expressed and integrated to help us clarify, find resolution and cultivate wisdom.

You see, journaling provides a safe and free space to have what we will refer to here as the epiphany—that moment where something that was previously hidden becomes clear. Through written expression, understanding begins to blossom, integration of this understanding begins to create wholeness, and embodied wisdom begins to form. It is through this embodied wisdom that we find much of our resolution and our way forward.

Journaling is often resisted, perhaps because it has the ability to cut to the core of an issue. This kind of work, like anything that is of lasting benefit, has a tendency to get pretty messy before it gets clear and comfortable again. Fortunately or unfortunately, this messy, vulnerable bit is an inevitable and vitally important part of this process, and it's always going to suck a little bit. There's no sugar-coating it. Journaling in this way can feel scary because we have a sense that once the emotional floodgates open, the chances of closing them again are slim. Ironically, once we do allow these emotions to be acknowledge and expressed, they often shift quickly and leave us feeling more peaceful than when we began. The trick, then, is getting courageous and even curious about the potentially uncomfortable space between opening your journal to write and closing it again at your completion.

There are no rules in the world of journaling, other than those you make for yourself. As a form of expression, it is its own art form, unique to you and your needs. All you require is something to write on and something to write with.

Here are a few journaling ideas to get you started...

1) Write a love letter to your animal.

Begin with Dear _____ (your pet's name). Express your feelings for your beloved furry friend and about how you are experiencing their final transition. Be honest, be upset, be hurt, be however you feel.

2) Just free-form it.

Journal whatever is in your head and/or heart at the moment. Let it all flow out of you and onto the page. If nothing comes, just scribble or doodle until a few words or a few paragraphs make their way onto the page. This can be an enlightening experience, showing you a whole new perspective that you may never have considered and often highlighting feelings, beliefs or fears that you may not have even known you had. As these arise, allow the thoughts to move to their natural conclusion and, if inspired, let your words map out a potential healing path.

3) Journal from your animal's perspective.

This is incredibly interesting stuff. In this way of journalling, you'll be writing your journal entry as if you were your animal. Your entry might begin a little like this: Dear _____ (your name) or Fabulous _____(your name) or Hello there, _____ (your name). After this, allow the words to flow without censoring, as odd as they may sound or feel. Go with whatever comes up. You can also ask questions like: What would you like to share with me about life/ connection/death/gratitude? You will often find a greater sense of clarity and understanding about what your animal is experiencing, or what you think they are experiencing. You can also do this exercise for animals who have already passed on, with the result being an incredible perspective about their experience through their transition. Very often you will be blown away by what you write down!

4) Draw it out.

Sometimes scribbling, doodling, drawing or painting can be a potent way of opening the doors to trapped emotions and unprocessed experiences. Find some crayons, paint or other medium of your choice and allow yourself to create, with no agenda. Notice what emotions arise as you are doing this, whether it be judgment, frustration, anger, sadness or something else.

Creativity can be an incredible pathway to greater healing, integration and vibrant living. The more that you include creativity in your life in any of the countless forms it takes, the more vibrant and inspired your life will become, and the more capable you will be of navigating the inevitable twists and turns of life.

So, there you go. A few very solid reasons why journaling rocks and why it would be awesome to give it a go. Don't underestimate this tool due to its simplicity—it has the potential to shift your life in great ways. With just a little courage and a willingness to traverse the depths of your emotions and stories, we can deepen our connection to the bigger picture, to our animals, and to this great adventure we call life.

The beauty of bodywork

Do you love massages? If you said no, then we really need to find you another massage therapist. Here's the thing—I have only met a few animals who, after getting used to the idea, didn't love getting a massage. And after spending over 12 years massaging horses for a living, I should know! In fact, animals and bodywork are a match made in heaven, somewhere up there with chocolate and peanut butter. I've found no better way to connect with our animals. Bodywork is not only an opportunity to connect physically, but goes much deeper, cultivating trust, acceptance, love and a depth of relaxation, circulation and awareness that is hard to rival. During an animal's final transition, bodywork can add significantly to the quality and, potentially, length of their life—a worthwhile payoff, for sure. And regular bodywork can mean the difference between knowing how our animal is feeling, quickly detecting when they are out of balance and understanding what they need in terms of support, and being out of the loop and trying to catch up.

The term bodywork casts a rather large net, encompassing everything from acupressure and massage to Bowen Therapy to the Tellington Touch Method to hands-on Reiki. It includes basically anything that is done by putting our hands on our animal. There are some cool things about this kind of work. First, it is often relatively simple and easy to learn, especially when it comes to working with our own animals. Second, it is the perfect practice for staying present, something that we're working on anyways (right?). And third, there are many benefits for our animal and their health.

Check out some of the awesome benefits to doing bodywork with your animals regularly:

1. Increased longevity
2. Improved circulation
3. Decreased pain
6. Calmer nervous system
7. Enhanced immunity
6. Greater connection between animal and owner
7. Increased relaxation and reduced tension levels

Learning about and employing some form of hands-on technique with our animal can, quite literally, change our relationship. For animals in nature, grooming and preening each other is a natural process. When my mare, Diva, first came into my life, bodywork was the bridge that connected us after other methods had failed. To this day, she will back into me to get a bum massage, placing me at the exact location for maximum relaxation and pleasure. This behaviour has understandably unnerved a number of non-horsey folks who find themselves on the receiving end of a bum-rub request from my unabashed 1300-pound Percheron-cross mare!

And on our end, the mere act of touching our animals can bring incredible comfort and a sense of connection. Far too often, we live in a world almost devoid of loving touch. The mere act of scratching, petting or cuddling our animals can feel like drinking fresh water after walking parched though the hot desert. It replenishes our need for connection and gives us a deeply satisfying sense of mutual enjoyment. It is no wonder we're attracted to petting and touching our animals. This simple interaction is remarkably comforting on both sides of the equation.

You might be wondering how you can apply the benefits of regular bodywork to your animal's final transition. The reality is, there are going to be more aches and pains as your animal ages. Just as with us, their body also begins a process of deterioration. Thankfully, this can be significantly slowed by the right supplements and food, and by bodywork designed to increase circulation and blood flow, remove stagnancy, balance the cranio-sacral rhythm, align the spine and generally cultivate vibrancy and flow in the body. Regular bodywork can significantly decrease the amount of discomfort an animal experiences and greatly enhance their quality of life, not to mention their longevity. You may decide as your animal ages, or just as a part of your health maintenance routine, to add a professional massage therapist, chiropractor or acupuncturist to your team. There are many incredible practitioners who have been trained to specifically improve the health and comfort levels of animals.

Want to learn some basic bodywork that you can do with your animal? You're in luck! I had a lot of fun working with Liam the dog during this video where I show several easy-to-learn canine massage techniques (http://bit.ly/massagedog). I have also included books, videos and other resources at the back of the book to continue your exploration of this fascinating and multifaceted area of health.

Building this connection with our animals during their aging process serves many functions, from the creation of a deeper understanding of our animal's state of well-being to an enhanced intuitive ability and a transformed perspective. And adding to our support team in this area is a powerful way to ensure we receive the help and guidance we need during this challenging time. On that note, let's talk about how to build our perfect team...

Building your perfect team

Nobody said that all the tools in our tool kit need to be all our own, or that we're meant to traverse this territory solo. The most successful and happy people in the world have one very important thing in common: the ability to ask for and receive support. Yes, it takes some vulnerability and the willingness to admit that we can't and don't want to do it on our own. As my dear friend and coach Tad Hargrave likes to say, we need an embarrassingly large amount of support to move gracefully through the inevitable twists and turns of life, and there is absolutely no shame whatsoever in admitting it. In fact, the sooner we do, the easier and more grace-filled our life is going to be, and the more open our heart will become. And that's always a good thing.

Let's take a moment to think about Batman and Robin. Not just because they look so good in tights, but also because they are the great example of a well-functioning team. Batman, even though he is a super-hero with incredible superhuman powers, still needs Robin. He doesn't feel weak asking for Robin's opinion or support in saving the world one bad guy at a time. He knows his team is a huge part of his success and that every super-hero needs a great sidekick.

For some reason, despite our distinct lack of Bat-mobiles, skin-tight suits (ok, I've got one or two) and disguising (but not too disguising) masks, we expect ourselves to do everything without help. If we really got down to the truth behind our need to do it solo, my hunch is it would have to do with the following:

First, we hate feeling vulnerable and admitting that we actually can't do it all ourselves. Asking for help, especially if we have BS filters telling us that asking for support is weak, feels like an admittance of defeat. Second, we might be feeling a sense of lack that is blocking us from moving forward, whether it be around money, time, love or energy. And the third reason goes even deeper. We really don't feel we deserve or are worthy of the kind of support that we want and need. And we hate the feeling of owing anyone for anything. So often, and rather defeatedly, we settle for just getting by with what we already have.

The irony is that the vulnerable and scary feeling of not-enoughness leads us to a tricky situation where we have no choice but to be enough—and way more. It's a conundrum, to be sure, and is often a self-fulfilling prophecy that ends in shame, guilt and the affirmed belief that we are, in fact, not enough (which is about as far from the actual truth as possible). Regardless of our particular blocks to asking for help, it's essential that we develop a supportive team and move beyond our limitations in this area—before, during and after our pet's inevitable final transition. Period.

When it comes to being terrific at handling transitions, creating a support team needs to be at the top of the priority list. A team member can be anyone in a supportive role in our life, and can include family, friends, colleagues and health-care professionals. Our trusted support team members are the ones we can call on in times of transition and at other times too. When we are falling apart, these are the people that have got our back. Here are a few questions to consider:

Who is on your support team at the moment?

Do you feel supported by and trusting of your team?

Do you know what you really need and want from your team?

If you have resisted the idea of having a team, then you may never have taken a moment to ponder these important questions. As the stewards of our animals, we get to make the call about who we want in our corner when stuff starts getting tough. If a specific team member is not meeting all of your needs in a certain area, that's fine, but what or who do you need to fill in the gaps? Do you need to let someone go and add a new player? In the particular context of death and dying, do you need a veterinarian who is able to make home visits? Do you need someone to help confirm the timing of this transition and support you in making the final call?

I know we're talking about our animals here, but let's not forget about you! I have witnessed countless animal lovers who book their animals in for a monthly massage and weekly acupuncture, and have them on a daily regime of health supplements and the best food money can buy, yet when it comes to their own self-care, fall way short. No guilt required here. We all do this on one level or another. In my lifetime, I have been notoriously bad at self-care, but enough episodes of burnout and a blown disc turned that train around. Now, I receive two massages a month and regular energy work as part of my routine, not to mention a self-care routine of baths, smoothies, yoga, dancing, hiking and scheduled-in time to cultivate relationships with an essential part of my support team—my best girl friends. These gals are there for me when shit hits the fan (as it inevitably does), and boy, I sure do need and appreciate their support.

Here's the thing. Even booking one massage a month can be an effective way to release stress, build your capacity for navigating challenging times and cultivate a mindset of self-care. You and your well-being are a priority—especially as the steward for your animal. It is essential to build a team for yourself even if you currently believe your animal or someone else is the main priority. Why? Because when you feel better, that rubs off. And you'll see the changes in your animals right away. This is why I work on animals AND their people! You, in more ways than one, are a package deal, whether you like it or not.

So, take a quick minute to get clear. What or who do you need to feel healthy and vital, and to allow the challenging transitions in your life to get easier and easier? Ask the same for your animals. Are they feeling supported by their current team? I mean, do they really like them, at least a little? Trust your gut response on this one. If not, what action do you need to take to build a team that truly supports you?

Remember, you are always a vital part of your own team. There might be a technique, modality or system that you can learn or build your knowledge around to be more supportive to yourself and your animals. Check out the modalities listed below, research your interests, take a course, or talk to other members of your team to find out how you can become a more informed and empowered animal owner.

Here is a list of some of the tools I love and use regularly:

- The Emotion Code (book by Dr. Bradley Nelson)
- Emotional Freedom Technique
- Acupressure/Acupuncture
- Tellington Touch Method/TTEAM
- Essential Oils
- Vibrational remedies and flower essences
- Animal Communication
- Homeopathy

Conclusion

During the inevitable transition of death and dying, one thing remains true: we are where we are. This means that wherever we find ourselves—in whatever emotional state, in whatever phase, and holding whatever perception—is exactly where we need to be. Expecting ourselves to experience death and dying as peaceful and berating ourselves when we feel something else is harmful and unnecessary. Our animals are happiest when we are just being ourselves, wherever we are in that moment. They don't care if we're in the messy middle, if we're deep in our grief or if we just feel numb to it all. Their love for us is unconditional, with space for all of our authentic experience. So often, in trying to fake happiness or pretend that we are OK, we forget ourselves and our own needs. We may actually need to run outside screaming, or write an entire page of expletives in our journals, or sob for a little or a long while. We may also need to ask for some help and support to hold us while we move through this challenging time.

Be willing to be as honest with yourself as you possibly can during this process. What do you feel? What do you need? What are just your stories, and what is the truth? Just asking these questions will transform your experience into something completely different. Getting real with the answers can be painful and you may find there is resistance to answering the questions. After all, you have been trained a certain way your whole life. But you can definitely teach an old dog new tricks, as our animals constantly show us. There will be hiccups and obstacles, but I encourage you to see them as opportunities for learning and growth, a chance to experience a new perspective on death and dying, and carve your own unique path to resolution and peace. Remember, your beloved animal will stay with you, in your memories of that special thing that only he or she did, and the way they loved and connected that was uniquely theirs and yours. You'll find your peace in that spot in your heart that's forever occupied by your unwavering love and appreciation for what they brought to your life. This is the expansion, the growth that comes through an ending and through inevitable transition—the heart grows and cracks open.

Death can be many things: an end, a beginning, an opportunity, a tragedy, an opening, a closing, a loss, a completion. Explore what it is to you, beyond all the programming and training, beyond culture and logic. And always remember to check in with your precious heart and with amazing animals. You'll be very surprised at all the amazing things it knows. I can't wait to hear what you learn.

It's been an absolute pleasure walking with you through these pages. If you're here, at the end, you are a serious trooper—you're willing, you're ready, you're open, and I'm digging it. It's also a good indication that you got a thing or two out of our time together, which is very cool. Your animals are deeply grateful for your commitment, as I am.

Happy trails and many blessings on your beautiful journey, and give your furry loved ones a snuggle for me.

To your fabulousness,

xo
Alexa

Want to keep learning?
Sign up for my free and very fun Furry Guru E-course at (http://bit.ly/furryguru). It's a fun and enlightening 5-day adventure all about discovering what the animals in your life would tell you if they could talk.

Or just come on over to www.alexalinton.com and connect. I'm quite literally an email away. Isn't technology cool?

Great Resources

Books

Rising Strong
  by Brene Brown, PHD
The Biology of Belief
  by Dr. Bruce Lipton
Energy Medicine
  by Sabina Pettitt, DTCM
Hands-on Healing for Pets
  by Margrit Coates
Communicating with Animals
  by Margrit Coates
Learning their Language
  by Marta Williams
Die Wise: A Manifesto for Sanity and Soul
  by Stephen Jenkinson
The Language of Miracles
  by Amelia Kincade
Straight from the Horse's Mouth
  by Amelia Kincade
The Emotion Code
  by Bradley Nelson
Power vs Force
  by David Hawkins
The Tapping Solution
  by Nick Ortner

The Tellington TTouch: Caring for Animals with Heart and Hands
by Linda Tellington-Jones

Videos

Excerpt from *The Animal Communicator* Documentary
http://bit.ly/animalcommunicatorvideo

One with the Herd Documentary
by Lisa Lightborn-Lay
http://bit.ly/onewiththeherd

Cortices Technique with Alexa
http://bit.ly/corticestechnique

Canine Massage Demo with Alexa
http://bit.ly/massagedog

Full Breathing video with Alexa
http://bit.ly/fullbreath

TTouch demo for senior dogs
http://bit.ly/ttouchforseniordogs

The Meaning of Death short film
with Stephen Jenkinson, created Ian MacKenzie
http://bit.ly/meaningofdeath

Audio

Grounding visualization with Alexa
http://bit.ly/groundingvisualization

Hydration Visualization with Alexa
http://bit.ly/hydrationvisualization

Meditation with Bradley Morris
http://bit.ly/bradley-breath

Online Courses

Kinetic Communication for Animal Lovers with Alexa
http://bit.ly/kinetic-communication

Bellyfit Embodied Goddess Program
http://www.bellyfit.com/embodied-goddess

21-day Meditation Program with Bradley Morris
http://bradleytmorris.com/meditationmakeover/

The Modern Day Cowgirl 21-day Bootcamp
http://alexalinton.com/mdcbootcamp

Notes

Meet the Author

Alexa Linton is a lifelong animal lover, leading her to a career spent working holistically with animals and their favourite people to cultivate balance, well-being, communication, and understanding. Over the past 12 years, she has supported thousands of animals and people as a healer, teacher and author. As an animal intuitive and energy medicine practitioner, she has been blessed and honoured to be present for many animals before, during and after their final transition. She adores doing one-on-one sessions with animals and their people, supporting them holistically through this transition and in all areas of their lives, which she offers over the phone or Skype. She graduated from the University of Victoria with her bachelor of science in Kinesiology, before following her horse obsession and becoming an Equine Sport Therapist and Animal Intuitive.

She lives with her crew—her horse Diva, dog Kia and cat Parker—in the Cowichan Valley on beautiful Vancouver Island, and spends her time frolicking in the rainforest, going on cowgirl adventures with Diva, dancing wildly and eating really good chocolate.

Learn more at www.alexalinton.com.

187

Meet the Contributing Authors

Bradley T. Morris

Bradley helps creative, entrepreneurial freedom-seekers, who are on a seriously awesome mission to share their gifts, serve the world, and build a meaningful business that aligns with their passions, to get clear, intentional and focused so they can create what they want in life.

He lives in paradise on a small island with his wife, Celeste, and is actively pursuing his lifelong dream of playing professional golf. Learn more at www.bradleytmorris.com.

Celeste Morris

Celeste is a Grief Enthusiast who helps women feel safe, confident and connected through the experience of healthy self-exploration, self-expression, self-love, sisterhood and sacred practices that honour the wholeness of life and grief.

Moved deeply by the need in our society to hold grief as a normal and sacred event, Celeste is impassioned to share what she has learned and hold space for women like you to embrace the great tides of grief that are a natural part of life. Learn more at www.celestemorris.com

Praise for Death Sucks

"As an Animal Communicator and a Medium who has done hundreds of connections with all types of animals here in the physical and in the Spirit world, this quote that Alexa writes in her book is the one that touches my soul: "Each one brings their own gifts, sharing with us their knowledge of tribe, transitions, grace or unconditional love." Alexa's perspective on the transition process for animals reminds me of how much we can learn from these beautiful creatures each and every day if we just take a moment to listen.

If you seek a greater understanding and one of honouring the beauty of our animal companions, then I highly recommend *Death Sucks*. Alexa makes a significant contribution to all animal guardians with her book and in every aspect of her work. It is an honour to know Alexa and to have read her book!"

—Diana Lynn Beatty, Psychic Medium, www.diana-lynn.com

"*Death Sucks* is a beautiful book with support for anyone who has lost an animal they love. Alexa Linton shares insight and perspective about this inevitable phase of the life cycle. Treasured pet companions can teach us so much about life, and transitioning through death is no exception. They help us to access parts we would like to keep hidden and they do so bravely. Thank you, Alexa, for this thoughtful guidebook for grief."

—Karla Kadlec, Sageheart Healing Arts, www.sageheart.ca

"I am very proud of Alexa for sharing her experience, life and tools to deal with one of life's difficult situations in a book like this. I have been in the situation many times of trying to relay to an owner that their horse (or other animal) actually wants to go. This book is a definite must if you are facing, or have just gone through this transition. I have no doubt that this book will change your life."

—Dave Collins, Founder and Head Instructor, BC College of Equine Therapy, www.equinetherapy.ca

"As important a book for animal lovers as all the guides on behaviour, care and feeding. This holistic and heartfelt exploration of death will assist the animal kingdom to share and teach through the transition at the end of their (not accidental) shorter lifespan. Death has always been one of our animals most important gifts. As that doorway between the worlds opens, our animals show us a deeply natural way of understanding life and death and this book is the illumination we need in the darkness of our grief. Thank you Alexa for your light."

—Laura Bird, Healer, Teacher, Communicator & Translator, www.onespirit.com.au

www.ingramcontent.com/pod-product-compliance
Lightning Source LLC
Chambersburg PA
CBHW031839090426
42741CB00005B/294